Women and Sports

Women

Janice Kaplan

and Sports

The Viking Press

NEW YORK

796
KAP

Acknowledgments

This book was researched under a grant from the Murray Fellowship at Yale University and written, in part, during a stay at the MacDowell Colony. Warm appreciation to Patricia Berens, Maureen Rolla, and Pat Irving for their support and encouragement, and to Ray Robinson for his early and continued interest. Also, thanks to William Zinsser, who, like it or not, taught me how to write.

First published in 1979 by the Viking Press
625 Madison Avenue, New York, N.Y. 10022

Published simultaneously in Canada by
Penguin Books Canada Limited

Library of Congress Cataloging in Publication Data
Kaplan, Janice.
Women and sports.
1. Sports for women. I. Title.
GV709.K36   796'.019'4   79–9777
ISBN 0–670–77837–0

Printed in the United States of America
Set in Videocomp Compano

With love to my parents

Contents

Foreword

I earnestly wish to point out in what true dignity and human happiness consists. I wish to persuade women to endeavor to acquire strength, both of mind and body.
—Mary Wollstonecraft, 1792

The first time I interviewed Chris Evert she was eighteen and so was I. She had just helped the American team win an international tennis competition (the Wightman Cup) and was talking about the thrill of victory while I waved a CBS microphone in front of her. Afterward, we walked out of the press tent together and Chris paused in the sunlight, held out both hands, and asked if I liked the shade of nail polish she was wearing. It struck me as absurd that I wanted to talk about tennis and Chris Evert wanted to talk about nail polish.

I didn't always like talking about sports. Like many young women, I grew up believing that (1) physical ability wasn't very important, and (2) I didn't have any. My older brother would play Frisbee or softball with me in our backyard, but as soon as the games got too rough, I would run away. I was only a girl. Not until years later did it occur to me that if the "only a girl" excuse was unreasonable in most areas, it was probably gratuitous in sports, too. By circumstance, I began meeting and interviewing a number of women athletes. Some of them, like Chrissie E., spent a lot of time trying to prove that jocks can still be girls, but many were quite at ease in the role of conquering heroine. They walked with a swagger that suggested they were comfortable in their bodies—notably unlike the young women I knew who had always decorated their bodies but never fully used them. The first articles I wrote about women athletes were, I'm afraid, unabashedly obsequious. I was fascinated by these women who didn't run away when the games got rough, and who apparently knew something about themselves and about female potential that I didn't yet know.

My interest in sports has nothing to do with how the Yankees are doing or who wins the Super Bowl. I am decidedly not a fan. But I am intrigued when women confront a side of themselves that they have never before known. A century ago, Susan B. Anthony wrote in her feminist newspaper *The Revolution* that in the battle for equality, women need strong bodies as well as quick minds. Recently, at a physical fitness seminar in Berkeley, California, I listened while twenty people explained why they wanted to begin exercising. Most said they hoped to look better or lose weight or improve their cardiovascular system. One woman in her mid-thirties had a different idea. "I'm recently divorced, and I'm trying to restructure my life," she said. "I've finally realized that the mind can't do anything without the body."

Where consciousness-raising groups were vital in the late sixties, body consciousness raising is the necessity a decade later. The women's movement has rallied around vaginal politics: abortion, contraception, gynecological arrogance. But sports has been a stepchild to feminism, since the issue of who gets to play kickball with whom has never seemed to be quite worthy of political upheaval. But it is important, because at stake is how women view themselves in general. Despite an increased sexual awareness, many otherwise liberated women are still dismally divorced from their bodies. For example, when a friend of mine in New York moved into an apartment with her male companion, she stood helplessly by while he moved furniture, built bookshelves, and painted. "It's not that I'm dependent," she said to me when I grumbled about the arrangement, "it's just that I'm weak."

For my friend and for other women like her around the country, that weakness is beginning to change. The new awakening to women's sports isn't a fad; it's a movement intimately tied to women's deciding that they want to control their own lives. By getting in touch with their bodies and pushing themselves beyond expected limits, women are discovering that they can do more than they ever imagined.

Chapter One

The New Image

*To have that sense of one's intrinsic worth which
constitutes self-respect is potentially to have everything.*
—*Joan Didion*

Being a woman sportswriter brings unexpected assignments. One fall afternoon when I had just returned from a football game, I received a call inviting me to be a judge at the Miss Teenage America contest. I was not an obvious choice. In a foolish moment during high school I had entered the contest, but my interests had changed and now the only time I wanted to see a girl pose in a bathing suit was after she'd set a new record in the Olympics. My phone contact hastily explained that Miss Teenage America needed a new image. My threats to give the title to a weight lifter didn't alarm anyone.

I expected to see little more than plastic smiles and baton twirling during the national finals in Dallas, but after interviewing all forty-three candidates, I was the one who was smiling. It was going to be difficult to pick a winner who *wasn't* involved in sports. Attitudes had changed in recent years—it was not only all right for a Miss Teenage America to be active in sports, it was almost required. One politically active Texan named Lolly Hatcher confided that she spent an hour every day training with weights at a local gym, then ran a few miles. "I do it to tone my muscles and because it makes me feel so good," she said. "Guys think I'm kidding, but I've really gotten strong."

ter Lolly came a parade of swimmers, divers, and hikers. One
dge asked a slim sixteen-year-old swimmer if she worried
about developing an athlete's shape. "I think it would be nice
to have broad shoulders, because it shows you're dedicated,"
she said. The only teenager I characterized as prissy was a
blonde from the Midwest who received my lowest score of the
day.

"What do you do when you're angry?" asked a judge.

"I don't get angry," she replied.

"Did you ever hit anyone?"

"Of course not," she said sweetly.

Later we met informally, and she mentioned that she loved
sports, played forward on her school's basketball team, competed in softball and swimming, and hoped to be a physical
education instructor after college. Looking at her carefully
curled hair and the legs crossed at the ankles, I asked if she
didn't find the aggressiveness of sports unladylike. "Not at all,"
she said, and for the first time there was a twinkle in her eye.
"I mean if you elbow somebody on a basketball court or give
her a bloody nose, you just remember that it's only a game."

The image of the ideal American woman is changing, and
activities that were once suspect are now admired. Nobody
laughs any more if a woman jogs around a park or dashes into
a supermarket wearing a sweatsuit. Being in shape is fashionable, and through sports, women are affirming their existence
as flesh-and-blood entities. "It's hard to think of yourself as
weak and dependent after you've just run two miles," says one
woman. This step-by-step coming alive through sports is causing a revolution in how women view their bodies.

Women's presence in sports is not new. Women in frilly
panties have been romping around tennis courts for a long time,
and one assumes that the bikini-clad Beach Party girls swam
around in the water for a bit when they got tired of chasing
Frankie Avalon. But what held women back, more than anything else, was their own image of themselves and the well-
learned precept that they should always consider how their

bodies looked rather than how they felt. "I think most women my age gave up on their bodies long ago and let ninety percent of their physical potential rot," says one woman who began jogging when she was thirty-six. "We ignored physical activity because we were always warned that a woman shouldn't demand too much of herself." Most women didn't bother testing their own strength because they assumed that they could rely on a man's. Girls were used to thinking of their bodies as someone else's property; they wore girdles and padded bras to make themselves appealing to men and never honestly considered how they felt about themselves. The antipathy to sports was particularly pronounced because athletics suggested an unnerving bodily confrontation. At a time when underarm deodorants were being frantically sprayed and jokes about B.O. set teenagers to sniffing themselves three times a day, who would purposely make herself sweat *more?*

Although the number of women participating in sports on all levels has skyrocketed during the past decade, old-time establishments have remained impervious to demands for equality. Intent on preserving their egos, men have tried to keep women out of sports for years. At the Harvard Club in New York City, some tradition-minded men were unhappy when women were first given membership rights. One alum expressed all the usual fears: that the women would faint from the rough language, drink too much and fall off a barstool, or try to put flowers in the steam room. A few blocks away at the Yale Club, the old Blues resigned themselves to opening the lounge area to women, then the bar and the men's tap room; but the swimming pool was another matter entirely. Using a ploy that has been repeated often in men's clubs around the country, the male members claimed that they always swam nude and so women could not be allowed to join them. Equality, yes; sports equality, no. Two female graduates who had been on the women's varsity swimming team politely requested that the men put on swim trunks one night a week. "Those women didn't stand a chance," a club member commented with a chuckle when the petition was denied. "Do you think the men would let in women who they knew were stronger and faster than them?"

Men sometimes seem more ready to accept women as brain surgeons than as athletes. Private golf clubs are notorious for maintaining "Male Members Only" rules during prime week-end hours, even though many women members also work full time. A typical attitude came to light during a 1975 press conference when President Gerald Ford mentioned his continued opposition to sexual discrimination. One unconvinced reporter asked the President how he could speak out on the subject and then continue to golf at the exclusively male Burning Tree Country Club. The President gulped. Fair is fair, he seemed to say, but why should his golf game have to suffer?

For the women athletes who began breaking down the male-only barriers during the past several years there was often anguish and humiliation—but there was also phenomenal success. The professional women athletes led the struggle, boosted by a surge in acceptance of sports among more typical women. It was a simple matter of dollar sense. Nothing could be done about inequities in prize money until commercial sponsors were convinced that supporting women's sports was a reasonable investment. A few commercial sponsors like Colgate-Palmolive and Philip Morris (makers of Virginia Slims) were genuinely eager to help women's sports, but they weren't going to supply $100,000 tournament purses regularly out of altruism. The decision for Colgate to become the controlling dollar behind several women's events—including golf, skiing, and tennis championships—was a calculated risk on the part of David Foster, then chairman of the board, and was much challenged. Since Colgate's chief competitor, Procter and Gamble, had an advertising budget roughly nine times larger than Colgate's, Foster realized that the Colgate commercials on afternoon soap operas were getting lost under the P&G barrage. Seeking to differentiate his products from theirs, he chose to link the Colgate name with the usually maligned lady jocks.

Most of the executives who tentatively supported women's

sports in the early seventies had similar motives. This was big business, and if the investments didn't bring mass acceptance, the companies would bail out. But they had stumbled on a field ready to explode, and their dollars helped set off the boom. The initial expenditures were made charily, but they paid off for both the women and the stockholders. In 1970, the public relations director for Virginia Slims agreed to invest $40,000 in the women's tennis tour, partly as a favor to fast-talking Billie Jean King and to an old friend, one-time tennis champ Gladys Heldman. That first year, women's tennis wouldn't have survived without Slims. About six years and ten million dollars later, the question was whether the cigarette would have survived without tennis. The champion woman tennis player had changed from a slightly amusing aberration to a highly respected and very visible heroine. The cigarette's slogan—that American babes had come a long way—meant something special because of the tennis tie-in. When before in history had a woman been able to earn a respectable salary for her physical skills? At last women were being paid to use their bodies, and that didn't mean baring their chests at nightclubs or flashing their tails at Playboy parlors.

At Colgate, the corporate image makers began spending about five million dollars a year sponsoring and promoting superstatus affairs like the Colgate–Dinah Shore Winner's Circle of golf. Foster, an impeccable English-bred gentleman, would appear at the championship every year, get his picture snapped with bubbly Dinah, and hope that every housewife watching in Peoria or Dubuque would associate his products with the star's looks and style. Meanwhile, Dinah was becoming a nonthreatening missionary for women's sports, urging the women who watched her daytime show to become more active. As the editors of one women's magazine wrote: "Dinah sure is healthy. What's the matter with the rest of us?"

As the public response to the woman athlete grew more positive, Madison Avenue executives were quick to recognize the shift. They had often used brawny males like Joe Namath to lend machismo to possibly suspect products for men like cologne and fur coats. Then, in a curious twist, they began asking female athletes to endorse products aimed at women. Why bring jocks into ads for fragrances and cosmetics? "Women don't relate to do-nothing beauties any more," said one advertiser. "They'd rather identify with an energetic champion." The winsome Breck Girl might once have been an ideal, but now shampoo ads featured Chris Evert and Olympic ice skater Dorothy Hamill. A short, wedge haircut became known as the "Dorothy Do," and young athletes who had previously moaned about the practical need to keep their hair short suddenly discovered that they were in style.

Languishing models didn't totally disappear from advertising, but the moonlight-and-pearls approach to women became less pervasive. Advertisers began featuring sports motifs, urging readers to achieve a natural glow with the help of tennis rackets and running shoes. Of course, if the readers did what the pictures suggested, they wouldn't need to buy the blushers and lipsticks to achieve the "natural" look, but that fact was generally ignored. When the Bonne Bell company promoted a new fragrance called "Bonne" with a full-color ad showing a female runner in shorts and a sleeveless T-shirt crossing a finish line, her arms thrown triumphantly above her head, it was probably the first time that a young athlete's armpits were used to sell a fragrance. "There are a lot of girls now who are healthy and active and aren't afraid to sweat," said Jess Bell, the president of the company. "Anybody can look good at a party if she spends all day resting and putting on makeup. I'm more interested in the woman who leaves the party at ten-thirty P.M. so she can be up early the next morning to run." To prove that he wanted to attract the early-to-bedders of the world, Bell began a campaign for the company's astringent with the slogan "Exercise Your Body. Ten-O-Six Your Face." And instead of blushingly lovely models, he used his own wholesome-looking daughter and, in one ad, a picture of the start of the Boston Marathon.

Not all companies were quite so daring, but there was a

general recognition that the American woman wanted new role models. Designer Geoffrey Beene acknowledged the connection between vibrant femininity and sports by giving free samples of his perfume with each pair of monogrammed tennis shorts. And Margaux Hemingway, who was paid one million dollars to represent one of Fabergé's lines, stopped being a flirtatious ingenue in the ads and was depicted skiing, ice fishing, and snowmobiling.

The new image of athletics actually had a greater impact on average women than on the professional athletes. Not only were pros making more money than ever before, but women who had stopped climbing trees in fifth grade and remembered high school gym classes as a misery of cold showers and chartreuse bloomers were beginning tentative forays into physical activity.

Madison Avenue's exploitation of the glamorous side of women's sports had the felicitous effect of convincing some people that "woman" and "athlete" weren't contradictory terms. But there was a danger. With sports being promoted by the same people who brought women vaginal deodorants and hairspray, they seemed to be nothing more than a new fad to fit into the old mold. Instead of exercising to have fun or feel better, women were encouraged to shape up their bodies so men would take a look and linger. Gyms were advertising exercise classes with a Mark Eden sell: Gain inches in the bust! Lose them in the waist and hips! But something important—the liberation of the female body—was involved in all this; and once women began taking an interest in sports, they couldn't help rearranging their attitudes along with their figures. They didn't have to be champions to understand that involvement in sports does more than slim waists—it changes the total way of viewing the body. Certain champions annoyed some feminists by refusing to associate themselves with liberation doctrine. But their silences didn't particularly matter since their actions reverberated loudly, proving what women could do if they only dared to try.

While women were progressing and gaining professional recognition in fields like law and journalism, their advancement in sports offered particularly dramatic examples of female power. For instance, it became harder to maintain the cultural stereotype of female fragility when women were playing contact sports, or to believe that women lacked stamina after 1967, when Kathrine Switzer entered and completed the then male-only Boston Marathon. "I didn't know it was illegal for a woman to run there," says Kathrine now. "I thought that other women just weren't interested." She had been training with members of the men's track team at the University of Syracuse and registered for the race as K. Switzer, her standard, androgynous signature. At the starting line, the team members all packed together, dressed for the cold, rainy weather in baggy sweatsuits and hoods. But when Kathy began to warm up a few miles down the road and pulled off a layer of sweat clothes, an official named Jock Semple suddenly realized that a girl wearing makeup and earrings was running in the crowd. He chased her down the road, trying to rip the number off her back. "He was really going bananas, and I was terrified," says Kathy. "I acted like a girl and burst into tears." One of her teammates—a 220-pound man whom she later married and divorced—knocked Semple away, allowing Kathy to finish the race. She became an instant celebrity when newspapers across the country featured her on the front page, but not everyone was overjoyed with her accomplishment. Officials of the Amateur Athletic Union suspended her from their ranks, declaring that women weren't allowed to run more than one and a half miles. "It was unbelievable," says Kathy. "Here I had just done something which they were saying was impossible, and they wouldn't change their minds about it."

Male officials might have been able to ignore the obvious, but many women began to understand that the established guidelines on what they could do were simply wrong. With Kathrine bounding up to the starting line of every long men's race she could find, wearing neon green sneakers, matching hair ribbons, and short dresses, it was difficult to pretend either that women were incapable of running or that runners couldn't be pretty. By the time the AAU changed its regulation in 1971, a lot of women had received Kathy's message. What had been a handful of women competitors turned into a horde, and when L'eggs pantyhose sponsored a six-mile race through Central Park in 1978, more than four thousand women stampeded toward the finish line.

Participation by women in marathons and other races soared; many of the runners were born-again athletes who at age thirty or so had begun to wonder what their limits really were. Among the runners at the L'eggs race were a few grandmothers, a seven-months-pregnant woman, and several jelly-thighed novices. "This is a lot more satisfying than playing hopscotch," commented one woman at the race who crossed the finish line with her daughter. Added another: "I was the kind of little girl who played with dolls and pushed baby carriages. You might say this is the first real challenge I've ever had." At stake was a much bigger issue than how many miles a woman could pound her feet over pavement. "Girls had always been told not to express themselves physically, but once we started, the whole world changed," says Kathrine. "I never quit during a race because I sometimes felt like I was holding up all of womankind and people were just waiting to point a finger and say 'See? Of course the girl can't make it.'" But the girl can.

Women like Gloria Steinem and Betty Friedan have been speaking for a long time on the untested limits of female ability, but the evidence that women are amassing for themselves is more convincing than the polemics. "You look back over the miles and miles you've run and think, I did that! My little body!" says Kathrine Switzer. "You never feel the same about yourself again." That sentiment is being echoed all over. A young gymnast from Connecticut named Leslie Russo soared to championship status when she became the first American woman to do a double back flip. A waiflike teenager who explodes with power when she performs, Leslie is happiest when she's learning a new trick. "It's neat seeing all the stuff you can do with your body," she told me shyly during one practice session. "You hear about a trick and figure that you can't possibly do it. Sometimes it takes two weeks or a month or maybe longer to get it, but when you do, it's like flying." Sports euphoria is hitting women hard. It has become more difficult to get tennis courts on weekday mornings, when all the mothers are out playing, than during the traditional peak times, when male weekend players appear. In big cities, squash rackets and Adidas bags get lugged to work along with briefcases, and in suburbia, jogging has replaced coffee klatches as a prime method of socializing.

Getting involved in sports is, for most women, far more than a symbolic assertion of female vigor and possibility; once she has done the impossible in sports, why not in everything else? Once they find their place in the sun through softball and volleyball teams, local football leagues, and neighborhood competitions in everything from skateboarding to sailing, women free themselves from sexist demons and realize that assertiveness training comes easy with a bat and ball. "Most women have a lot of self-doubt and built-in masochism," says Dyveke Spino, coach to several Olympic athletes and codirector of New Dimensions in Lifestyle, based in Boston and San Francisco. "They don't really own themselves, and they don't know how to go into the world and grab what they want." Instead of pep talks or consciousness-raising groups, she uses physical activity to put women in touch with their inner power and make them realize that much of their energy and vitality has been untapped. A middle-aged woman who runs eight miles every morning up and down a mountain, Dyveke was trained as a clinical psychologist but decided that provided a limited way of dealing with people. "I wanted to teach women to love themselves and get in touch with their feminine energy," she says. "You can't deal with the mind and emotions unless you pay attention to sports and games. Remember the Greek ideal which talked about the integration of mind, body, and spirit? Well, you get strong mentally while improving your body, and the whole psyche opens."

Many of Dyveke's protégées insist that the sense of self they gain through sports transfers to other dimensions of their lives. Several have changed jobs, gotten out of bad marriages, or gone back to school. "Sports give you a beautiful sense of who you are," says Dyveke. "Women always look for external acclaim, but through sports the values start to shift to a natural, inner joy. Instead of painting on some glamorous image, you discover your own inner vibrancy. And every bit of the glow you feel is real because you've created it yourself by exploring the limits of your body." When Dyveke gives workshops around the country to introduce women to her methods, she often gets a crowd of nonathletic women running around a gym in high spirits for nearly two hours. At the end, they're always shocked to discover that the blonde shaman in black leotard and sneakers has had them galloping several miles. None of the women can explain the magical spell that Dyveke casts. One overweight psychologist who met her at a seminar in Los Angeles remembers giving Dyveke a big hug at the end of the session.

"I've never felt like this before," she said. "How did you know I could do it?"

"You just needed some encouragement," said Dyveke.

Later, the woman began working regularly with Dyveke and lost most of her excess weight. She has thought often about that mysterious first session. "Something about Dyveke's attitude made me lose my self-consciousness," she says. "I stopped thinking about whether or not I could keep going, and just enjoyed it. At one point I started to feel uncomfortable because I was sweating so much, but then Dyveke said, 'Think of it as a cooling waterfall. It's beautiful! Your body is delightful when it's taking care of itself!'—and I just accepted that."

Dyveke is always quick with such affirmations. "I look at an overweight woman and I know that in some ways she doesn't really like herself. She needs to get some sense of her personal worth before she can reorganize her life. If I can make her see that what she does with her body is really under her control, then she can begin to change."

The message that sports can bring joy to women's lives has spread rapidly. Sporting-goods companies report that their fastest-selling item is running shorts, and most attribute the booming sales to the excitement generated by the women's sports movement. While most of the buyers wear the track shorts for exercising, the briefs have also become a fashion item. Instead of asserting her upward mobility by wearing a Chanel suit, a woman can do the same by slipping into five-dollar cotton track shorts. The Paris couture houses began picking up on the active image in 1975, and fashion reporters at the Paris openings stared disconcertedly at models wearing sneakers. The designer playclothes were mostly unaffordable fantasies, but they relayed the message that the stylish woman wanted to be unshackled. In 1978 designer Karl Lagerfeld said he had created his collection for "women with real bodies" instead of stick-slim models who looked as if they never lifted anything heavier than a silk scarf. Other unlikely people began getting into sports. Stewardesses from every major United States airline, eager to prove that they could do more than smile and serve coffee, tried serving tennis balls at an international stewardess tennis tournament. And at the Madeira School, an exclusive girls school in Virginia, the headmistress decided to send her charges off once a week to a program called Discovery, which gives courses in backpacking, rock climbing, and outdoor survival. "At first we figured we'd all be killed and never get to our debutante balls," says one former student, "and then we realized it was really the debutante balls that were killing us."

In a recent poll of *Seventeen* magazine readers, three of the top five women listed as "Most Admired" were athletes—quite a change from the late sixties when the older sisters of the current readers invariably voted for romantic actresses like Olivia Hussey and Ali MacGraw as the most admired. Even the ubiquitous high school cheerleader began to lose some of her status when girls saw that they could grab their own spotlight rather than settling for reflected glory. Standing on the sidelines for a game or a lifetime does not appeal to women who understand that they can drop their pom-poms and be more than the women-behind-the-men. "I feel better when I'm being cheered than when I'm cheering," says one young woman who quit her school's drill squad to show horses. "My whole personality changes when people are looking up to me because I'm doing something special." Even male traditionalists have found more to admire in talented women competitors than in their giggling adulators. Apparently success has enough charm to win popularity contests. Lusia Harris, a 6'3" black basketball center from Delta State, was elected to reign as queen over her school's homecoming court; and Shirley Babashoff got her school's crown after winning Olympic medals in swimming. "The competition's getting rough," said one of her classmates wryly. "It used to be that a nice smile was enough. Now you have to get a gold medal to be appreciated."

This acceptance of lady jocks has taken years to evolve. For a long time it seemed clear that girls had babies to prove that they were women, and boys had footballs to prove that they were men. So why should a woman get involved in sports? Changing the pattern was frustrating, and some of the biggest controversies centered on wholly symbolic issues. For example, otherwise reasonable men were torn apart by the ego-involving question: "Should women get varsity letters?" When the matter arose at the University of Michigan, members of the M Club, all letter-holders, banded together in a movement to keep women out of varsity-letter sweaters. It was a curious fight, since nobody challenged the fact that the women on the newly formed varsity teams were training hard and competing in full schedules. "But that has nothing to do with whether or not they're athletes in the same sense that we are," said one M man. Another member insisted that if a girl wanted to wear a letter sweater, she should find a boyfriend who could give her one. An official of the club sent a letter to all alumni members, explaining that once women started running around in letters they had won themselves, the M would lose its meaning. "I didn't know that M stood for male," snapped one of the shunted females. An administrative Solomon finally resolved the controversy by designing two different Ms—large ones for the men and small ones for the women. The move seemed to reflect the opinions of Paul Weiss, a professor of philosophy at Catholic University in Washington, D. C., who wrote in 1969 that men should think of women as "truncated males" who can participate only in foreshortened versions of the men's games.

But women athletes are not little men, and at the 1977 National Women's Conference in Houston they became symbols of consummate womanhood, paradigms for women who want to use their bodies and minds without embarrassment. Several weeks before the event, a torch was lit in Seneca Falls, N.Y.— the site of the first women's rights gathering in 1848—and over two thousand women joined in running with it to Houston. Wearing T-shirts emblazoned with the motto "Women on the Move," the women passed the torch relay-style to herald their physical and symbolic arrival. At the Texas border, twelve uniformed sheriffs on horseback, all carrying flags, paraded behind the runners and escorted them to a ceremony where they were given a key to the city. "We've had to run pretty hard to get some doors open," cracked one woman. In most areas along the torch route, the women were greeted with accolades and saluted by local officials as the torch passed from housewives to high school students to Olympic athletes, each woman carrying it for one mile. But there was still some heckling and obduracy along the way. Just as the torch was approaching Alabama, more than a dozen runners decided to withdraw from the relay, saying it was widely rumored locally that all the women running were lesbians and against prayer in the schools. Nobody could convince them otherwise. But the renegades couldn't spoil the symbolism and flow of the procession, since a young runner named Peggy Kokernot flew in from Texas to cover the sixteen-mile gap between Birmingham and Clampton.[1] Other problems were also handled with flair. Right before an important rally in Washington, D.C., the flame went out, and nobody could find the wicks needed to relight it. "We've always succeeded by female ingenuity," someone proclaimed, proceeding to stuff the brass tube with Kotex, ignite it, and go flaming into the conference.

During the last stretch of the relay, the official runners were flanked by female athletes, politicians, and celebrities. Bella Abzug, the outspoken politician from New York, ran in the entourage without even removing her hat. At age fifty-seven and caught in sprawling middle age, she was an unexpected ambassador for athletic vitality, but her presence was apposite. The thrill of watching oneself come alive at any age creates a self-confidence that is at the core of the women's movement. "Before we can change our mental image, we have to develop a better physical one," says Abzug. Most men are glad to peel off their shirts on a warm day and join a touch football game, no matter what kind of over-thirty bulges they reveal. Meanwhile, anxious women stay away, sure that they're too clumsy or lumpy or inept to join. Changing that negative self-view means an upheaval in social structures. Women who are no longer estranged from their physical selves, who realize that they're not fragile and don't need to be protected, are less likely to fall into culturally mandated sex roles. Without worrying about how a man is judging them, they'll use sports to feel good and be healthy.

That was the message as three young women clad in gym shorts finally carried the torch into the packed convention hall and were greeted with tears, shouts, and half-hysteria. "The

1. Peggy got her picture on the cover of *Time* magazine for her effort. Ironically, the same week that she ran the sixteen miles, the International Olympic Committee voted to ban women from competing in a 3000-meter race (roughly two miles) in the 1980 Olympics, calling it too grueling.

torch was meant to be a symbol which could unite all the women who touched it," said Pat Kery, one of the organizers of the relay. "When it actually worked out that way, it was overwhelming." Bella Abzug took the torch and presented it to the three First Ladies who were at center stage—Lady Bird Johnson, Betty Ford, and Rosalynn Carter. The sight of three conservative First Ladies, Bella, the liberal politician, and three young athletes all gathered around the sweaty runners' symbol inspired another impassioned response. Despite their clashing images, all the women on stage understood that there was no activity too vigorous for a woman and none that she should be denied. Now encomiums were being sung for women on the move, but who over twenty-five could forget the contumely that once would have been heaped on a woman running—with or without a torch? For too long women had assumed that they couldn't do much of anything that required strength. These women were gathered to proclaim that that just wasn't so.

Chapter Two

Physiology

First, be a good animal.
—*Ralph Waldo Emerson*

Much of the controversy about women in sports comes down to a question of bodies: male bodies and female bodies and what each can do. Men and women have different strengths and different points of vulnerability. Women are generally more flexible, agile, and balanced than men; men are taller, heavier, and more muscular. But even generalizations like these are too simplistic, since there can be greater differences among the members of one sex than between the average man and the average woman. In sports, as elsewhere, it's vital to treat men and women as individuals and not just as members of their sex. Surely Lasta Semenova, the Russian woman's basketball star who weighs 281 pounds and is over seven feet tall, has abilities different from those of an 85-pound gymnast. Dr. Jack Wilmore, head of physical education at the University of Arizona in Tucson, insists that women are more restricted by social constraints than by their own capabilities. "A woman who's encouraged in sports can perform enormously well," he says. With some of that encouragement beginning to appear, women are setting athletic records once considered beyond their reach.

A woman's alienation from her own body begins about the time of her first period. Physiological changes take place then, to be sure, but they're minor compared to the effects of the moralizing that's dispensed with every box of Tampax, the warnings that it's time to come inside and start being a woman. I remember the first time I walked into a women's locker room where some pro athletes were cooling off; I was surprised because the women were all sitting around nude. Why weren't they ashamed of their bodies like the rest of us? From junior high on, we hid behind towels after gym class and avoided taking showers. In seventh grade, we spent several weeks seeing films with titles like "Babies and You," which showed a lot of animated pictures of eggs. The boys, who clearly had nothing to do with reproduction, were off playing football while we sat quietly in a darkened room, learning how to guard our bodies. Mysterious things were happening, and we had to be careful.

What everyone forgot to tell us was that the mysteries would be much easier to take if we stayed in touch with our physical selves rather than being scared by them. Ask women athletes about sex, pregnancy, and menstruation and they invariably say they feel great during all three. Compared to sedentary women they are (1) more interested in sex, (2) half as likely to need a cesarean delivery, and (3) less affected by the phases of the moon. But the great myths about sex and sports haven't yet been effaced, and women continue to worry that sports will be damaging. The vague, half-conceived fears are generations old, passed on by grandmothers who insisted that a girl should preserve her body for reproduction and nothing else. In one sense the grandmothers were right in associating sports with sex—young women who learn through sports what their bodies can do are unlikely to be sexually passive or ashamed, a fact that may be alarming to some women but a real breakthrough for others. "The fear used to be that vigorous exercise would make a girl lose her virginity," says one gynecologist. "I assume that means it would perforate her hymen. I've rarely known that to happen, but I think most girls now would be relieved rather than upset if it did."

Menstruation

Most women over twelve may think they are quite well-versed in the intricacies of menstruation, but virtually no adequate studies on the subject have yet been done. For example, why do some women suffer severe cramps (dysmenorrhea) every month, while others experience absolutely no physical sensation? It's likely that most of the Victorian ladies who spent two days every month throwing up from their periods had mental rather than physical distress to blame, but nobody is really sure. "If men had cramps, we'd have a National Institute of Dysmenorrhea," says Dr. Clayton Thomas, a medical researcher and onetime physician at the Olympic Games. There *is* evidence that active women usually don't have much trouble with cramps and bloating. A woman who does get cramps might feel better if she ran a half mile or did some vigorous toe-touches; that usually is more effective than crawling into bed with a heating pad.

Women have won Olympic gold medals at all phases of their menstrual cycles. In various surveys, about 50 to 60 percent of the women athletes say they don't notice any change in their performance during menses. Of the rest, about half say they do worse and half say they do better. Much of this may be psychological, but the variations in blood pressure and resting pulse rate that occur in some women may have some effect. Despite the inconsistencies in women's reactions, men often advise women not to compete or take important tests when menstruating. They hint that a woman may *feel* fine during her period, but subtle furies are stirring that leave her without much control over her own body. Unnerved by this possibility, some athletes have tried taking birth control pills to avoid menstruating at inconvenient times. "I've trained too many years to lose a world championship just because my period falls on the wrong day," says one woman. But the cure may be worse than the problem. The high levels of estrogen in birth control pills can make a woman less energetic and possibly upset her stability and timing.

Dr. Robert Brown, a psychiatrist associated with the University of Virginia, thinks exercise can prevent premenstrual blues. He contends that one cause of depression is a chemical imbalance, caused by a buildup of sodium in the body. Some antidepressant drugs like lithium are chemically almost identical to sodium and may work by replacing the salt in the body. "You can ease salt and water retention before menstruation by taking a pill or by working up a good sweat," he says. Dr. Brown conducted an extensive study with women students at Virginia to see the effects of a high-exercise and low-salt-diet plan on menstrual problems. Nearly all of the women who tried the plan said they felt considerably better when they exercised and cut down on salt for about five days before their periods. The exercise and sweating not only raised spirits, it eased premenstrual symptoms like tender breasts and backaches.

While the amount of blood a woman loses during her period —about two to four ounces—is relatively insignificant, it can hamper athletic performance by depleting the iron supply. The phrase "iron-poor blood" that pharmaceutical advertisements have made famous isn't totally misleading. Women store only a small amount of iron in their bodies—about 250 mg (as opposed to 850 mg for men). Iron is needed to synthesize hemoglobin, the compound in red blood cells that does most of the work of carrying oxygen to the muscles. Women generally have a lower hemoglobin count than men anyway, and if it's further depleted by menstrual loss, the ability to utilize oxygen during exercise suffers. The solution is rather simple: an over-the-counter vitamin supplement with iron.

Taboos and amulets for menstruating women may be relics of antiquity, but where sports and menstruation are concerned, the calendar got stuck centuries ago. At one Catholic girls school in the Midwest, the students are not only allowed to excuse themselves from gym classes once a month, but required to do so. "We will not permit amusement that might interfere with procreation," says the director of the school. And in California, women who want to compete in authorized professional boxing matches must sign a statement that, to the best of their knowledge, the contest won't take place during a menstrual period. Nobody in the boxing commissioner's office could explain that regulation, except to say: "We are aware that women are different from men."

Even among the more liberated, worries about menstruation still exist, and stories about unexpected periods seem to inspire undue embarrassment in the tellers. For example, one woman in her late twenties remembers playing tennis once at a snobbish club in Brookline, Massachusetts. "We were playing on court number one—closest to the clubhouse—even though the management isn't fond of having women on the good grass courts," she says. Club members were lounging on the terrace with their cocktails, and she didn't mind being watched, especially since she was beating her male opponent. "We were almost finished when some club official walked over and told me to default the game. I didn't know what the hell he was talking about, but he kept rambling on about women and decorum. I went to the ladies' room, and sure enough, I'd gotten my period and my panties were soaked through. I wouldn't go near the club for weeks. Then I realized that I was being ridiculous. Getting your period is not one of the great evils." Once, at an international fencing tournament at the New York Athletic Club, a sixteen-year-old competitor asked permission to wear her warm-up pants over the all-white fencing suit. "I wish girls would stop thinking that they're different on days when they have their periods," said Julia Jones, an elderly woman who is a member of the fencing Hall of Fame and who was watching the proceedings. "Even in my day, I understood that menstruation isn't worth worrying about."

One question that has not yet been answered is why many athletes who train strenuously stop menstruating for several months or years, and some who begin training very young reach puberty noticeably late. When Dr. Dorothy Harris of Pennsylvania State University wrote about this phenomenon in a women's magazine, she was inundated with letters from young gymnasts, swimmers, and skaters whose periods had either ceased or never begun. The only pattern that Dr. Harris noticed in the letters was that many of the women had never had regular periods to begin with, and others had begun a stringent diet at the time they began exercising. Dr. Kenneth Foreman, a physical education professor at Seattle Pacific University, studied the top female long-distance runners in the country and found that 17 percent of them had irregular cycles, ranging from periods less frequent than once every forty days to no periods at all. His findings were similar for gymnasts and long-distance skiers. From questionnaires distributed at the Olympic training camp in Squaw Valley, Dr. C. Harmon Brown of California State University concluded that about 30 percent of the runners had no periods at all during intensive training. One theory about all this is that in distance athletes and in gymnasts, body fat drops to about 12 percent of body weight or lower. This may be too low to support pregnancy, which could explain why the reproductive system gets turned off. A similar phenomenon occurs among young women whose weight drops dramatically from physical illness or anorexia nervosa. But other doctors strenuously disagree with this theory. "Low body fat certainly isn't the cause," says Dr. John Marshall, the director of sports medicine at the Hospital for Special Surgery in New York. "It may be that the delicate balance of hormones gets upset from certain kinds of training—or it could be psychologically induced from the stress of workouts and competition." Other stresses—from broken love affairs to long airplane rides—are also known to cause menstrual disturbances.

When some of this evidence was first reported, a male coach said to me: "It's just as I always thought—sports turn women into men." That's hardly the issue. In fact, the case is similar to one uncovered when researchers at the University of Helsinki in Finland tested male marathon runners. They found that the men's level of testosterone fell after a race—which generally means that the sperm count is also lowered. The exact effects of that are yet unknown; however, nobody has thought to conclude that running turns men into women. None of the doctors who have been looking into menstrual problems among athletes believes that exercise or competition can permanently impair fertility. Regular ovulation begins again almost immediately when the rigorous training is eased, and trouble-free pregnancies can follow. "I don't yet have the answer as to why the amenorrhea occurs," says Dr. Harris, "but I strongly doubt that it's harmful in any way. It may just be the best form of birth control we've found."

Birth Control

Whatever other advantages or disadvantages they may have, the simplest methods of birth control are also the safest for women athletes. There's nothing in a diaphragm that could possibly disrupt sports performance. Not so for the IUD. Many women report that their menstrual flow becomes so heavy with an IUD that the bleeding is bothersome during a long game or race. Also, there have been reports of women whose IUDs slipped from rough body contact—a hard field-hockey check, for example—and on rare occasions this can result in a punctured uterus.

Contraceptive pills may also be inadvisable for many women. Common side effects like bloating and weight gain are clearly detrimental in sports. Pills with a high dosage of progesterone can sometimes cause sluggishness. Large amounts of estrogen are even more harmful and may sap energy and lower endurance. Male athletes have been known to "dope" themselves with shots of male hormones like testosterone for extra strength, but nobody ever took estrogen for the same purpose.

Women who take the pill are about three times more susceptible to heart attacks than other women, and women who smoke and take the pill increase their risk of heart disease ten times. "We used to think that women were practically immune to heart attacks," says Dr. Lenore Zohman, a cardiologist at Montefiore Hospital in New York, "but that's just not true any more. Now women do all the same things as men—we smoke more, we're overweight, we're into high-stress jobs, and on top of all that, we have all the complications and dangers from the pill." Dr. Zohman urges women who insist on taking the pill to begin regular aerobic exercise programs to reduce their risk of heart disease. Aerobics are activities like bicycling, running, or swimming that raise the pulse rate for an extended period of time and so improve cardiovascular fitness. Aerobic exercises can help neutralize the raised blood pressure that the pill causes in some women. They also lower the resting pulse rate—which means that the heart is working more efficiently and pumping the normal amount of blood with fewer strokes. The pill is a major risk factor in heart disease, and exercise is a major means of prevention.

Pregnancy

The first time most people heard of all-girl rodeo was when Sue Pirtle Hays rode bareback broncs in a world championship when she was eight months pregnant. Reporters who didn't know a bronc from a bull fell all over each other trying to find out why the twenty-two-year-old cowgirl from Oklahoma was committing such folly. Hays explained that even though she was one of the top riders in all-girl rodeo, the money on the circuit was so bad that she couldn't afford to miss the lucrative world championship, no matter what. "It was a little tricky trying to balance two people instead of one on a bucking horse," she said afterward, "but my doctor agreed that there was no reason not to enter. Really, people have a lot of misconceptions about pregnancy." Her bouncing baby, Ty, was delivered healthy and on schedule the next month.

Riding wild horses is not a recommended activity for most pregnant women, but then, it's not recommended for most people at any time. The key for active women during pregnancy is:

Keep doing whatever you're accustomed to. Hays's doctor advised that the jolting ride wasn't likely to disturb the pregnancy, and even if she were thrown from her mount (which she wasn't), the fetus would be well protected by the sack of fluid that surrounds it. Only a strong kick in the stomach from her horse would have had noticeable consequences—though probably doing nothing more than inducing early labor. Hays decided that since she had never been kicked before, she wouldn't worry about it then.

Starting a vigorous exercise program during pregnancy isn't advised, but women who are in shape before becoming pregnant and continue their regular activity for as many months as feels comfortable are likely to feel good and have an easy time delivering. The scare stories about how activity can cause miscarriages are best ignored. About one in four pregnancies ends in miscarriage (sometimes before it's even known that the egg was implanted) for reasons that have nothing to do with sports. Very few miscarriages occur because of external stress. Dr. Clayton Thomas says that, generally, a strong egg will remain intact and an unhealthy one will spontaneously abort. According to the laws of natural selection, it makes sense that the healthiest women will have the healthiest babies.

When tiny marathon runner Miki Gorman became pregnant for the first time at age thirty-nine, she stopped training for three months, worried about the possibility of a miscarriage. But by the fourth month Miki, who normally weighs under ninety pounds, was feeling so sluggish and heavy that she began running again, and she continued running every day until a week before her daughter Danielle was born. "I was so fat then," says Miki, a delightful Japanese woman, "that at the end I was only running a mile a day, and they were ten-minute miles." After the birth, she took about a month to recover—about normal for active women—and returned to her normal weight almost immediately when she began running again. Her speed also returned quickly. Before Danielle turned two, mother Miki ran the fastest race of her life, winning the women's division of the 1976 New York City Marathon.

Exercise can alleviate complications of pregnancy like high blood pressure, headaches, and swollen ankles, and well-conditioned women often have the easiest and fastest deliveries. A study of several hundred female athletes showed that close to 90 percent were in labor for a shorter time than average, and they had 50 percent fewer cesarean deliveries than the average population. "My doctor had warned me that I might need a cesarean because I'm so small," says a Florida woman, "but I'm really strong from swimming and doing sit-ups and lifting weights. I begged him to let me try natural childbirth, and everything went fine. I have tight stomach muscles, so when he said 'Push' I really knew how to help my baby along." Worries that vigorous exercise will suffocate a fetus are groundless. The developing baby gets fed oxygen before the mother, so even if the woman is out of breath, the fetus is probably well supplied with air and nourishment.

Most women athletes I've spoken to say they felt comfortable exercising until roughly the sixth month of pregnancy. One cross-country skier actually worked out just hours before her baby was born. She had found that running a few miles eased the pains of pregnancy, so one day when she was feeling particularly squeamish, she ran four miles. It didn't occur to her that she was having labor pains. Stories like that are common among cowgirls in the West who, like Sue Pirtle Hays, keep riding their horses or working in the fields until it's time to go to the hospital. One Colorado rancher told me that she was hitting tennis balls against a backboard four hours before her baby arrived. "I'm hoping it will make her a better tennis player," she said, grinning. "You know, there's nothing like starting a child early in sports." Still another American woman, Juno Stover Irwin, won an Olympic medal in diving, competing on the ten-meter board, when she was in her fourth month of pregnancy. Plunging the equivalent of four stories into a swimming pool while the whole world watched didn't hurt the child a bit.

Mothering

More than half of the Soviet women medal winners at one recent Olympics were mothers—which suggests that the real problem for American women isn't whether their bodies can get back into sporting shape after pregnancy (they can), but how to find the time to exercise between changing diapers and feeding the baby. Physically, becoming a mother isn't any more detrimental to sports performance than becoming a father.

Many women find that their performance improves after childbirth. Tennis players Margaret Court and Evonne Goolagong both assumed that they would slow down after becoming mothers, but it didn't work out that way. Court had her first baby in 1973 when she was thirty years old, and in the year that followed, she won over $200,000 on the tennis circuit. It was her best season ever, and in one stretch of her comeback, she won twenty-four of twenty-eight tournaments. "I never seemed to tire," she says. "I'd win one week and be ready to play just as hard the next week." Goolagong, a graceful, curly-haired Australian, returned from her pregnancy five pounds slimmer than before and stronger than ever. At first, she insisted that her maternal desires were so strong that she didn't want to leave her daughter, Kelly, and compete. But she found a solution better than quitting, and pretty soon Evonne was answering questions at postvictory press conferences with a towel draped around her neck and Kelly perched on her lap. When asked once why she seemed even more powerful on the court than she had before her pregnancy, she pointed to her little girl and explained that carrying around Kelly was like being on a constant weight-lifting program.

So many women have become impressive athletes after becoming mothers that one doctor calls pregnancy "a nine-month conditioning program." Some women find themselves particularly accident-prone immediately after giving birth, but their equilibrium is usually restored before too many pulled muscles and sprained ankles occur. Cathy Rigby, for years the best gymnast in the country, is a blonde sprite who became an actress and commentator for ABC-TV after she stopped competing. Married to former pro football player Tommy Mason, she had her first baby when she was twenty-three. A few weeks after leaving the hospital, she was scheduled to appear on the TV show "Six-Million-Dollar Man," playing a Russian gymnast. "I was worried because I had to do a balance-beam routine, and that doesn't leave much room for error," she says. "I had done stretching exercises and sit-ups the whole time I was pregnant, so it didn't take me very long to get back in shape. Everyone says the show was fine, but it certainly wasn't the best routine I've ever done."

Some of the best ballerinas in the world have had children during their prime dancing years—among them Melissa Hayden, Maria Tallchief, and Allegra Kent. Lately, Natalia Makarova, the premiere ballerina who defected from Russia in 1970, returned to the stage three months after her first baby was born. She claimed that the experience had brought a new richness and maturity to her dance. Natalia was dancing well into her fourth month, when her current dance partner, Rudolph Nureyev, stopped during a rehearsal to ask if she was pregnant. When she said yes, he nodded happily and continued the practice.

Women sometimes use childbirth as an excuse for getting fat and slowing down. Actually, it's a good reason for doing the opposite, since pregnancy inspires an increased body consciousness. After Miki Gorman had her child (her twenty-hour labor was a notable exception to the usual quick delivery among athletes), she wondered how anyone could say that women weren't strong enough to run marathons. "If women can have babies they can do anything," she says. "I say: Compared to having a baby, a marathon is easy!"

Mixing sports and babies hardly qualifies as a newfangled feminist practice. One of the greatest women tennis players from the early part of the century, Hazel Hotchkiss Wightman, did it without any regrets. Hazel was a short and stocky champion who initiated the Wightman Cup tournament, an annual British-American competition. She won the first of her forty-four national titles in 1909 and had the first of her five babies in 1913. At that point she had been unbeatable for three years. After beginning her family she played less—taking time out now and then to have her children—but kept winning. When she was nursing her first baby, she played Mary Browne, that year's national champion. Hazel won, 6–3, 6–0. Another time she was scheduled to play a match at 3:00 P.M., which was when she was supposed to nurse her baby. The match was moved to 3:15. "I never thought of my children as handicaps," Mrs. Wightman told me shortly before she died at the age of eighty-seven. "I enjoyed them and kept them with me. Being a mother doesn't have to limit you. I always brought one or two children to my games. They'd play very nicely on the edge of the court, and when they got a little older, they'd even watch me." She wrote her one book, *Better Tennis,* while waiting to pick up her children after school.

Hazel Wightman was admired around the world—the Queen made her a Commander of the Order of the British Empire (one of the highest honors that can be conferred on an American), and she was served many other awards—but her lesson on combining sports and motherhood seems to have been forgotten in some quarters with the passing years. A few young mothers are having a harder time than ever participating in sports. For example, in 1976 a senior at Eads High School in Colorado decided that she wanted to play on the school basketball team. She had been the star of her team as a freshman but soon found other extracurricular interests, and by senior year she was married and had a baby. School officials told her that she couldn't play basketball any more, and when she complained in district court, she lost the case. But courts in Ohio, Oklahoma, and Iowa have realized that having a husband and child doesn't necessarily fill every moment or satisfy every ambition in a young woman's life, and have therefore ruled that banning mothers from the playing fields is unconstitutional.

At a recent track meet in New York, an eighteen-year-old unmarried mother took advantage of these decisions and prepared for her race while her younger sister sat with the baby on the sidelines. It was the young mother's first competition ever, but she was calm. "My life isn't over just because I have a baby," she said. "My body's in good shape, and I have a lot more respect for it now. I hadn't played sports before because I was too busy running around with boys. Now I know better, and I figure that God made my body for other things than just having babies."

Body Structure

When the law allowing girls to play on Little League teams was passed in New Jersey, several coaches were so irate that they quit their positions. The coaches didn't have to worry that including girls would mean fielding second-rate teams, because the law said that the girls had to try out for the teams the same way that the boys did. If the pigtailed players weren't good enough, they'd never make it to first base. Or the outfield. But after watching some practices, the coaches realized that many of the girls were better than the boys. The fact seemed a sacrilege to them. The rule of the playground—and the tenet of Little League—had always been that boys got to show off while girls admired. But now players named Amy and Linda and Marie were coming up to bat and slugging home runs, and medical authorities were insisting that this wasn't an aberration but an expected result of physiology.

If anyone is going to get hurt when boys and girls play together, it's just as likely to be the boys. At Little League age, about eight to twelve, girls are an average of two inches taller and four or five pounds heavier than boys. But when the Little League controversy began in 1972, hysterical parents were dragging in all sorts of "evidence" as to why their little darlings would be damaged for life if they ventured onto the same fields as boys. Afraid of destroying the macho myth in sixth grade, the adults began raising a lot of ridiculous questions. What if a girl got hit in the chest? Was the coach expected to rub the injury as he would on a boy? And what if she got hit between the legs? One antigirl petition signed by scores of parents expressed perturbation at the thought of a girl sliding into third base and being tagged out by a boy whose mitt could land anywhere. Even on her crotch. Nobody stopped to consider that it would hurt a lot more if *her* mitt landed on *his* crotch.

So many horror stories were bandied about that the New Jersey state education association asked former football coach and orthopedic surgeon H. Royer Collins to study the issue. After listening to the parents' agitated tirades and studying the medical data, Dr. Collins said that there was no practical reason to keep girls on the sidelines. The no-girls clause in the league charter just reflected the traditional and unwarranted linking of sports with manhood and the conviction that a girl's body must remain inviolate and untouched. The truth is that a female's reproductive organs are so well protected that injuries to the uterus, tubes, or ovaries resulting from sports are practically unknown. When Dr. Allan Ryan of the University of Wisconsin perused the medical literature, he could find only three cases where reproductive organs had been damaged through sports. In each of the instances, the injury was the result of a waterskiing accident. Since the danger is in vaginal injuries caused by the intense water pressure of high-speed falls, Dr. Ryan recommends rubber wet suits for fast-moving waterskiers.

Actually, it's surprising that there haven't been more accidents among women in sports, since protective equipment for women is hard to find. Women on some amateur football and ice hockey teams have taken to wearing pelvic protectors, equivalent to male jock straps, which have been dubbed Jill straps. But things like shin guards, ice hockey skates, crash helmets, and even sneakers are almost always designed for men, and ill-fitting equipment can be dangerous. Dr. LeRoy Perry, a chiropractor who works with many of the top athletes in the country (including baseball's Los Angeles Dodgers), says that structural stress problems can often be traced to bad equipment. For example, a woman who needs a pair of running shoes or basketball sneakers quickly learns that the men's shoes she has to buy are about one and a half or two sizes larger than what she's used to. (A woman who normally wears a size 8 will wear a 6 or 6½ in a men's sneaker.) But the problem is that a woman's foot is usually narrower than the men's shoe last. Two pairs of socks and tight lacing are the most common solutions, but that means that the arch support isn't in exactly the right place, the foot is probably flopping around too much, and there can be stress on the ankles, knees, or lower back. Perry often builds orthopedic supports into athletic shoes for women. "Look, it's a simple engineering problem," he says. "You want an athlete's body to be straight, like a skyscraper. And if you build a skyscraper on a weak foundation, what's going to happen? You end up with the Leaning Tower of Pisa, that's what."

Now that there's clearly money to be made in the women's sports market, more companies are considering women's special needs. Most of the major companies now make women's tennis shoes, and running shoes are becoming somewhat easier to find. One of the larger sports store chains is Herman's World of Sporting Goods, with stores all over the East and Midwest. Herman's managers report that about 40 percent of the business in the stores is from women, which should be a strong incentive for the buyers to stock more women's equipment. But often manufacturers confuse women's special needs with vanity. Many of the tennis rackets labeled "Ladies" haven't sold well, simply because the regular rackets were better designed and available in light and small sizes. Pink racket covers were not a major enticement to serious women players.

Sexism often takes the form of misplaced concern over protecting women's delicate bodies. While mysterious links between sports and breast cancer are often hinted at, no connection has ever been found. "It's a bunch of malarkey," says Dr. Dorothy Harris. "Having girls in basketball or field hockey wear chest protectors or padded bras is ridiculous. The breast tissue is soft, and it can be moved without damage." Still, when women began applying for boxing licenses, most state commissions decided to turn them down, piously noting that fragile breasts should be treated with more care than is offered by a gloved fist. The Amateur Athletic Union also barred women from boxing on the same grounds, and doctors on both sides of the controversy began compiling evidence that boxing would/would not cause breast injury. One doctor claimed that female breasts are a lot less vulnerable than most other parts of the body. He solemnly added that if the breast can withstand the maulings of love play and nursing children, it certainly can't be endangered in a boxing ring. "The real question is whether boxing is good for human beings, and the answer to that is no," says Dr. Harris. "But female breasts have nothing to do with it. It's not a problem." While male officials were fighting over this nonissue, female boxers found a solution in a specially designed aluminum-and-sponge-rubber bra. To prove that the breast debates were just so much hot air, a lovely boxer named Tyger Trimiar appeared on the Mike Douglas show wearing the bra over her shirt. Tyger has the large eyes and high cheekbones of a *Vogue* model, and she often appears in the ring at exhibition bouts wearing black velvet shorts and a midriff top. "But I'm serious about getting recognition and money for women's boxing," she says. "I had Mike Douglas hit me bare-fisted in the chest a few times to prove that the bra works. Now they'll have to find another reason to keep us out of the ring."

The subtler differences between male and female anatomy may be important to sports performances, but nobody yet knows exactly what is attributable to hormones (which tend to get blamed for everything) and what to social opportunity. For example, when I was a kid, I was told that it's an inevitable fact of nature that girls run and throw like girls—which of course means badly. But as I got older my throwing inexplicably improved. I found out that the only reason most girls throw funny or look uncoordinated when they swing a bat is that they rarely get the chance to practice.

One of the few people who have seriously studied the potential of women in sports is Jack Wilmore. Most physical fitness tests done in the United States have predictable results—the women do badly enough to fuel a year's worth of keep-'em-off-the-field arguments. But statistics can be deceptive and Dr. Wilmore remained skeptical. In one of his own studies, Wilmore found that prepubescent children of both sexes are about equal in many athletic skills—except the softball throw. Instead of assuming that girls are genetically programmed not to throw baseballs, Wilmore was puzzled. It didn't make sense that boys should be able to throw the ball twice as far as girls although boys weren't twice as capable at anything else. He tried the test again and had the kids throw the ball with their nondominant arm. This time the girls and boys performed almost the same. "The girls did poorly on the first test because they weren't used to exercising those muscles, and the boys were," says Dr. Wilmore. "The second test showed that, potentially, their abilities were very similar." In other words, the only reason girls "throw like a girl" is that they haven't practiced.

Fat

Even if their scales don't say so, most women are fat. Their percentage of body fat to lean weight is high—about 25 percent for average college-age women as opposed to 15 percent for men of the same age. Some of this is sex related. Boys lose their "baby fat" during adolescence, while girls acquire some fat then, most noticeably around the breasts. (It may be unromantic, but the female breast is most accurately described as a lump of fatty tissue.) But the fat deposits that women generally acquire on their hips, thighs, and upper arms don't necessarily have much to do with femininity.

Dr. Wilmore contends that what is accepted as normal body composition for women (22 to 26 percent fat) is probably too fat. Standard height-weight figures don't reveal much about body fat, since it isn't always related to total weight. A 100-pound office worker, for example, might have a higher percentage of body fat than a 145-pound athlete who is lean and muscular. In fact, since fat is lighter than muscle, women who begin exercise programs often notice that their clothes become too big and they look slimmer, but they don't weigh any less. This is one time when it's wise to ignore the scale. Lean body weight is firmer and sleeker than fat, and it doesn't sag or jiggle.

When Wilmore analyzed the body compositions of women who were long-distance runners, he found that their fat values were about half those of sedentary women. Most of the runners had less than 15 percent body fat, and many of them were as low as 6 or 7 percent. These low percentages were a result of training, Wilmore believes. One of the women in the group had started running because she was overweight; she liked running so much that after her weight dropped, she began training seriously. When Wilmore encountered her she was a world record holder and had only 6 percent body fat.

There's a connection between levels of body fat and levels of androgen or estrogen, so while a woman can probably reduce her body fat considerably, she might never get as lean as a man who trains with her. With this in mind, it's nice to know that while fat isn't beautiful, it can occasionally be useful. Fat floats, and it offers insulation from extreme cold (which is why more women than men survive blizzards)—a good combination for long-distance swimming. Women have been very successful at feats like swimming across the English Channel and hold most of the records for endurance swims. As long ago as 1926, Gertrude Ederle, then eighteen years old, swam from France to the cliffs of Dover faster than any man had ever done it.[1] Her feat was so inspiring—and her time so

1. Ederle's time was 14 hours, 31 minutes. The current women's one-way record is under 9 hours.

remarkable—that when she came home to New York, she was feted with a ticker-tape parade. Almost fifty years later, another New Yorker, Diana Nyad, decided to set her own record by swimming around her hometown, Manhattan. A few people suggested that it would be easier to walk on the Harlem River than to swim it, but Diana, whose last name means "water nymph," was determined. On her first attempt she ended up in the hospital, exhausted and almost lifeless from the cold, but a few weeks later she tried again and managed to slosh through the twenty-eight miles of gop in less than eight hours, one hour under the previous record for that swim, set by a man named Byron Summers.

The water temperature for Diana's swim was 65 degrees, considerably warmer than some of the frigid crossings other women have experienced in the English Channel or Lake Ontario. The swimmers dive in wearing only a racing suit, goggles, and bathing cap; no other equipment (such as a fur-lined bathing suit) is permitted. "You use up about five thousand calories every hour in a swim like that," says Diana, "and no matter what you take during the feedings, you rely on your own body fat for energy and warmth. No amount of grease will protect you as well." Still, the swimmers do coat themselves with layers of thick grease—sometimes lanolin and paraffin, or axle grease, or maybe simply pounds of Vaseline. "It gives you a good feeling at the start," says Diana, "but it all washes away in an hour and you're back to depending on whatever you have inside."

Other women continue to astound with their marathon feats. When Canadian Cindy Nicholas staggered ashore in Dover before dawn one autumn morning in 1977, she had been in the water almost twenty hours. Cindy had crossed the Channel three previous times—enough to be used to the jellyfish, rough tides, and seaweed. But this time, after she swam from the cliffs of Dover to the French coast, she decided to turn around and come back. She completed the round trip an incredible ten hours faster than anyone else had ever done it.[2]

All this may be inspiring but not particularly useful, since most women don't lie awake at night dreaming about crossing the Channel. But a marathon swim demands the one quality women were always assumed to lack—endurance. These examples of fortitude by Nyad and Nicholas and others suggest that a woman's body has unsuspected reserves. People have generally believed otherwise; the first time women were allowed to run anything longer than a sprint in the Olympics was in 1928, and officials predicted disaster. The forecast was right. Eleven women entered the 800-meter race (about a half-mile); five dropped out before the finish, five more collapsed after crossing the tape, and the hardiest fainted in the dressing room shortly afterward. Officials banned women from running that distance until 1960, and even now the longest race for women in the Olympics is slightly under a mile. The anachronistic members of the International Olympic Committee insist that anything longer is too torturous for the weaker sex. The irony is that women actually do better in endurance events than in any others. The 1928 debacle was probably an example of women failing because they were expected to fail. None of them had ever trained for long distances, and they were psyched out by adumbrations of doom and the ambulance waiting at the finish line.

In most "supermarathons"—anything over fifty miles—women tend to show a special talent. For example, the first time Miki Gorman went to the Los Angeles Athletic Club she was thirty-three, and she ran a half-mile, then collapsed. Just a few months later she ran in the club's twenty-four-hour endurance race and completed eighty-five miles. The next year, she ran one hundred miles in twenty-one hours, stopping only to go to the bathroom and eat a little bit. Another woman who won a

2. Cindy's double crossing took 19 hours, 55 minutes, which is two hours less than it took an Englishman, Captain Matthew Webb, to make the first one-way Channel swim a century earlier.

fifty-mile race in California was actually going faster at the end than at the beginning. The explanation for these heroic deeds may be in body structure. Joan Ullyot, a San Francisco physiologist, thinks that women are able to use their fat as fuel. She got the idea from Dr. Ernest van Aaken, a well-known German biochemist and running coach, who feels that the body's supply of glycogen gets depleted before most people finish a standard marathon. The phenomenon of "hitting the wall" after about two hours of solid running probably occurs because all the glycogen in the muscles has been used. The runner suddenly feels excruciating muscle pain and continuing the race is about as easy as running through a closed door. Hoping to prevent this, runners often go on special "carbohydrate-loading" diets before an important race. But before one race, Dr. van Aaken told Ullyot that no matter how much applecake, pasta, or bread she ate, the stored carbohydrate couldn't last more than eighteen miles. Ullyot began checking with her fellow marathoners and found that none of the women she knew had ever experienced "hitting the wall." That doesn't mean they don't get tired—just that they don't experience the kind of sudden agony the men experience. Ullyot's latest conclusion is that women are able to utilize the fat in their bodies for energy almost as efficiently as both women and men use the glycogen formed from carbohydrates.

For those who think that's a good reason to indulge in banana splits regularly, Ullyot is careful to make a distinction between "trained-on" fat and "eaten-on" fat. The latter is dead weight and a burden to the muscles that have to carry it around. The fat that has been part of the body composition while the athlete trains is metabolically active, can be oxidized when needed, and therefore acts as stored fuel. Looked at this way, heavy muscles are an impediment for endurance events, since they're weight which can't be used for energy. Where muscle power is needed—such as in sprints—men will always have an advantage. But for long events, the woman's body is built for survival.

Sweat

There's some truth to the adage that horses sweat, men perspire, and women glow. A woman's body temperature has to be raised an average of two to three degrees higher than a man's before she begins to perspire. This may be fine for preventing under-arm stains, but it probably makes women susceptible to heat stress, since sweating is one way by which the body keeps itself cool. The best solution is not necessarily to sit under a sunshade and avoid all exertion when the temperature climbs above 65 degrees. The body generally adapts to the demands put on it, and Dr. Dorothy Harris suggests that if girls are encouraged to run and sweat when they're young, their bodies might become more adept at handling heat. A person living in the tropics, for example, has more sweat glands and better resistance to the heat than someone from Alaska. Similarly, a Southern Californian would have an advantage playing tennis on a hot, humid day against an opponent from Maine. It has also been conjectured that men are wasteful sweaters. A woman's vascular system brings more blood to the surface of the body to be cooled, possibly compensating for the smaller quantity of sweat. However, some women have difficulty dissipating heat in hot climes because they have a relatively heavy layer of subcutaneous fat (fat right under the skin)—the same fat that would insulate them crossing the Channel. Exercising enough to change the ratio of lean weight to fat may also improve the ability to handle heat.

Bones

Send a girl whooshing down a ski slope and she's likely to end up with . . . a broken leg? Boys and girls are nearly identical in bone strength before puberty, but girls stop growing at fifteen or sixteen, and boys continue developing until their twenties. The added years of growth permit more gradual ossification, which results in larger and heavier bones for men. But there's no need for women's bones to be quite as light and delicate as they often are. Just like muscles, bones get stronger when they're used. For example, in a right-handed woman, the bones in the right arm will be denser and more substantial than those in the left arm.

In both women and men, the skeleton can be strengthened by activity, since exercise keeps bones intact in two ways. First, when the tendons and muscles around them are firm, the bones are less susceptible to injury, and they are strengthened by the constant pulling of the muscles. Also, calcium is metabolized best when the muscles around the bone are being used and stimulating the blood circulation to the area. When a leg or arm is immobilized in a cast, the bones lose calcium and become light and porous—which is why there's always the danger of another break immediately after a cast is removed. Similarly, astronauts returning from a no-gravity setting in which they're floating free with no pressure on the skeleton often suffer from weakened bones for some time after they return.

Estrogen helps keep bones solid in young women, so the real danger of crumbling bones begins after menopause. The best way to stave off bone deterioration is by getting the bones strong through exercise—which also reinforces the tendinous attachments. It's not a coincidence that older women frequently suffer broken hips when they're confined to a wheelchair or nursing home. If they manage to keep walking and moving on their own, their bones are less likely to weaken and break.

Heart and Lungs

Women don't have notably big hearts, but size isn't always the best determinant of ability to function. Their smaller heart capacity doesn't make women tenderhearted—that is, they're not in danger of damaging their heart or lungs by overuse. In fact, the heart will get stronger and function more efficiently as it's used.

There are a number of ways of measuring cardiovascular fitness. One phrase that researchers bandy about is "VO_2 capacity," which refers to the volume of oxygen a body can utilize. It's often expressed in relation to body weight, because the more active tissue in the body, the more oxygen can be used. With training, women can improve their VO_2 by amazing amounts. One researcher found that young women who spent six weeks in intensive training for cross-country running increased their aerobic capacity by 20 percent. In general, the difference between VO_2 in trained and untrained women is close to 40 percent. Dr. Barbara Drinkwater, a research physiologist at the Institute of Environmental Stress in California, says that the best way to develop aerobic power is to participate in a taxing sport. Cross-country skiing, running, and speed skating will increase VO_2, while sports like golf and archery won't.

Comparing male and female aerobic power is deceptive, because once again, "average" men are apparently functioning closer to their potential than "average" women. For example, the oxygen uptake of a female swimmer is about 40 percent greater than that of an untrained woman, while a male swimmer's intake is only about 15 percent greater than that of a more typical man. Similarly, American and European sportswomen score about the same on all of the tests that measure ability to use oxygen, but among women who aren't involved in competitive sports, the American woman scores far below her European counterpart.

The maximum heart rate for most women is probably close to 200 beats per minute, although it declines with age. For a long time researchers thought it was far less than that, probably because women were rarely involved in sports that got their blood pumping. Resting heart rate for a woman in her twenties is usually 70 or more, but the rate will drop several points after just a few weeks of training. This drop reveals an improved stroke volume—an ability to send more blood through the body with a single heart beat. Women not previously accustomed to exercising will have dramatic improvement in cardio-respiratory functioning during the first few weeks of training. Unless they monitor their body systems closely, this won't be immediately obvious, but the eventual result is better performance and more energy.

Strength

At one Midwestern college, a 115-pound female undergraduate found out that a neighbor in her dorm was a national collegiate wrestling champion. One evening she asked the 160-pound champ if he'd like to leg wrestle with her. He agreed, and to the delight of everyone in the dorm who had gathered to watch, he lost.[3] It was one of the few bouts in which he was ever defeated. The vanquished wrestler walked around shaking his head for a few days and claiming that he was going to take up knitting. But he shouldn't have been that surprised. If you make allowances for differences in body weight, men and women have almost identical leg strength. Dr. Wilmore has found that when expressed relative to body weight, women's leg power is only 8 percent less than men's. In terms of lean body weight, women are 6 percent stronger in their legs than men.

Overall, the average man is almost twice as strong as the average woman. (He's also taller and so proportionately stronger: biological fact.) When highly trained athletes are measured, the difference drops precipitously, to about 10 percent. Wilmore contends that there's no reason why that gap couldn't be cut in half. Only a 5 percent difference in strength between men and women? When the editors of a women's magazine heard Wilmore's findings they blared a headline: "Pound for pound, you're as good as he is." The change from a 50 percent

3. In leg wrestling, opponents lie on their backs, head to toe, and raise the inside legs so they touch at the calves. At "GO," the point is to push hard enough on the opponent's leg to tip him over. This isn't a totally fair test of strength, since a low center of gravity and fairly wide hips often give women an advantage over men. For that reason it is a totally fair way for a woman to prove a point, or embarrass the machismo out of a neighbor.

difference to a 5 percent one involves more than statistical sleight of hand. "When you experiment with average men and women you are, in effect, comparing sedentary females to active males," says Wilmore. "That means you're measuring cultural, not biological, differences." American women aren't inherently weak—they just spend less time exercising than men do. The differences in upper body strength between men and women are enormous, and one reason for the similarity in leg strength may be that women naturally strengthen their legs by walking, climbing stairs, and biking—common activities for girls. But they don't do much that will strengthen their upper bodies. Years of climbing trees and tossing footballs give boys an advantage in arm strength.

Eager to prove that most women can be hardier than they ever imagined, Wilmore persuaded a group of female students at the University of California (where he was then located) to get their muscles working by embarking on a weight-lifting program. Seventeen weak-kneed coeds agreed to the experiment. They signed up for ten weeks, and by the end, the budding superwomen showed substantial increases in strength—often 30 to 50 percent. Having traded fat for muscle, they looked firmer and sleeker, even if the bathroom scales didn't register their triumph. In addition, while they built strength, they didn't develop bulging muscles. Muscular hypertrophy is related to testosterone production, so a woman can get powerful without getting massive. In other words, weight lifters aren't all that-way-to-the-beach muscle men who flex their biceps and pop their pectorals at every chance.

Jan Todd, an English teacher and farmer who won the U.S. Women's National Championship in power lifting, can heft close to 500 pounds, which makes her the strongest woman around right now. Her power would be impressive even for a man, since about 95 percent of all professional football players can't lift as much as she does. Jan broke a record for female lifting power that had been untouched for more than forty years—possibly because nobody had dared to challenge it. She has become an inspiration to women who wouldn't have suspected that an energetic blonde who quilts and who cans her own tomatoes could also perform such heroics with weights. Now many others are recognizing that women can get strong without turning into he-men, and increasing numbers of them are participating in competitive weight lifting. One year Nebraska officials tried to keep two college women out of the state championship by demanding that they weigh in nude. They did, and each won trophies. Enough women have caught the strength fever so that there are now women's championships by weight-class all over the country.

Flexibility

Strength is only part of the sporting equation. Occasionally, male athletes work so hard on building huge biceps that they're virtually unable to bend their arms. To be effective in almost any sport, it's important to strike a balance between strength and flexibility—even though the two sometimes seem mutually exclusive. That is, women who have no trouble doing splits and can contort their bodies into pretzel positions often can't budge a full suitcase or push a chair across a room. Those who have no trouble with strength events are likely to be so inflexible that they cringe at the mere suggestion of touching their toes.

Dr. James Nicholas, the director of the Institute of Sports Medicine and Athletic Trauma at Lenox Hill Hospital in New York and a consultant for several professional teams, explains this by dividing people into two categories: loose-jointed and tight-jointed. Being loose-jointed—a condition more common in women than in men—improves performance in sports requiring flexibility and impedes it in those that demand strength. Nobody is exactly sure why women are more likely than men to have this elasticity, though it may have something to do with hormones (as usual) and the fact that because women have less bulk, the connective tissues between their joints are thinner than those in men.

Dr. Nicholas has linked loose- or tight-jointedness to susceptibility to injury in various sports. A woman who can touch her palms to the floor with knees straight, sit lotus style, and do backbends is likely to be very loose-jointed and therefore vulnerable to popping kneecaps, shoulder dislocations, and ligament problems. A tight person may have more power and explosiveness, but she pays for it by being prey to muscle tears, strains, and pulls. As the orthopedic surgeon for the New York Jets football team (he won the monicker "Nick-the-Knife" for operating so often on Joe Namath's knees), Dr. Nicholas analyzed the incidence of injury among the players. He found that 72 percent of those he considered "loose" ruptured knee ligaments at some point. Only 9 percent of the "tight" players had the same trouble. Overall, the risk of a ruptured ligament is about seven times greater for loose athletes than for tight ones. You can't make a loose joint tighter, but you can protect yourself by doing exercises that improve strength and power. "Some of the finest athletes are in the flexible group," says Nicholas. "They generally have less muscle strength, but they might compensate with extreme maneuverability and quickness."

Finding out if you're loose or tight is simple. One do-it-yourself test is to grasp the thumb of one hand and try pushing it back to the forearm. If the thumb reaches (or almost reaches) the forearm, loose-jointedness is indicated. Another test: With straight wrist, try pushing the index finger backward. If it forms a ninety-degree angle or less with the back of the hand, it's a good sign of looseness. In that case, you probably have flatter feet than most and your kneecaps tend to float a little bit. This can lead to trouble in many sports unless you prepare yourself with some simple strengthening exercises. The problem is that if the quadriceps, or muscle in the front of the thigh, is weak, the knee joint lacks a firm anchor and is more likely to slip.

Similarly, the tibia and fibula, bones in the front of the calves, are connected to the knee and ankle by tendons and muscles. When they are underused and poorly developed, added stress is put on the joints.

Total fitness isn't possible in five minutes a day, but stronger legs and knees are. The best exercise for strengthening the quadriceps, and therefore the knees, is the straight leg raise with weights done while sitting on a chair. Instead of fancy equipment, homemade weights are fine. Take an old handbag, fill it with three or four cans of soup, and slip the strap over the ankle of the leg being exercised. Slowly raise the leg parallel to the floor and hold for a count of ten. If the handbag seems too clumsy, most sporting goods stores have weighted ankle cuffs or boots.

Because women generally have wider hips than men, the angle between the thighbone and tibia is wider—which leads to additional stress on the knees. Staying away from sports that exercise the legs isn't likely to prevent problems and may, in fact, cause them. For example, a loose-jointed businesswoman named Melissa who has never been very active in sports once managed to dislocate her kneecap walking out of the kitchen of her house. A few years later, she did the same thing at a formal dance—an unsettling scene for Melissa, her date, and the police, who rushed in, hearing that someone had collapsed on the dance floor. "It didn't seem fair," says her younger sister, "because I was always the jock in the family and Melissa was the one who ended up in a cast." Actually, it was probably her participation in sports that kept the similarly built and equally loose-jointed younger sister off crutches, since the knees are best protected when the surrounding muscles are strong.

Sports that seem to put the most strain on the knees may actually be the best for some loose-jointed women, since they exercise the neglected muscles. Abby Fisher, one of the members of the U.S. Ski Team, has trouble with slipping kneecaps, but the problem has never kept her off the slopes. "Abby weighs about a hundred and ten pounds," says John Marshall, the team doctor, "and I have her doing straight leg raises with ninety pounds for sixty repetitions." Similar exercises work for other problems. "I was panicked that I'd end up with heavy thighs from using weights," says a woman who, on doctor's orders, did thirty minutes of leg exercises three times a day when she was recovering from a broken left leg. "But it was amazing because after six weeks my left thigh was an inch and a half slimmer than my right." Weak muscles can also cause shin splints—tenderness and pain in the bone in front of the calf—which are common in women. They are often caused by the impact from running, skiing, or even walking when there's constant pounding on hard surfaces. In skiing down a mountain, for example, the pressure from gravity and acceleration may be about five hundred pounds per square inch. A basketball player grabbing a rebound comes down with a force four or five times body weight, and a runner imposes three times her body weight with each step. That force must be absorbed somewhere—by muscles, knees, feet, ankles, or shins. Everyone from ballerinas to parachute jumpers learns to bend his or her knees to reduce the jar of landing. If the muscles are strong enough, they can ease the shock by countering the pressure. Obviously, sitting behind a desk all week doesn't prepare the muscles very well for the impact of bouncing over moguls on a ski slope or even for cycling down a country path on the weekend. "Strength training really isn't that complicated," says Dr. John Marshall. "Think of it this way: When you lie in bed, the muscles relax and atrophy. So just walking around is some kind of strength development. Running is a little better. Working with weights or some resistance equipment is better yet."

Concern about women's knees and loose joints has often been used as an excuse for keeping them out of certain sports. But there are loose-jointed jocks on the male side who have excelled in strenuous sports, and their body type hasn't hurt their performance. Nobody ever suggested that Joe Namath or O. J. Simpson shouldn't play football, even though they're both loose-jointed, as are basketball stars Wilt Chamberlain and

Julius Erving. Many of these athletes have knees that seem to be held together by Band-Aids. If you already have knee problems but want to participate in a sport like tennis, basketball, or gymnastics that demands some agility, a knee brace might prevent further damage.

Pain and Injury

Many women who get hurt when they start a sport should probably blame their problems on fashion designers and beauty editors rather than on loose joints, genes, or hormones. The scorn directed against the whaleboned corsets of a century ago, which offered slim waists along with shortness of breath, languor, and pale cheeks, might well be turned now against high-heeled shoes and imported Italian boots. They regularly contribute to the pains in the feet, heels, and ankles that many women experience when they begin a sport. The sexy black sandals with the three-inch heel may look fine, but they destroy natural flexion. When the foot is constantly slanted from a high-heeled or wedge-heeled shoe, the heel cords and muscles in the backs of the calves tighten and shorten, and the tendons become contorted. In sneakers, the foot lands flat, as it's meant to, and pulls on the constricted muscles. So as soon as a woman accustomed to wearing high heels steps off her pedestal and tries running on a beach or field, the strained calf muscles and heel cords may rip or pull. High-heeled shoes probably aren't worth stabbing pains in your legs. One 5'1" woman who began running during a summer on Cape Cod says it took several weeks before her maladapted muscles could be stretched back into their natural condition. When she returned to the city, she traded her closetful of high-heeled shoes for flat Capezios. "I probably look better, too," she says, "because I don't mince any more or worry about stepping carefully. I may be short, but I just stride along."

Many of the pains that afflict women in sports are similarly unnecessary, and often the culprit is lack of information. For example, if nobody has told you to warm up before you run a mile or play two hours of tennis for the first time, there's a good chance you'll be hobbling the next day. But just how likely is it that a young woman will get really hurt during sports? In a survey of 125 athletic trainers, published in the *Journal of the American Medical Association,* only 3 percent thought that female athletes were more injury-prone than males. Many others agreed that when women enter competitive sports without sufficient training, skills, or conditioning, the chance for injury does increase. Improper treatment is also a problem for women, since there's a scarcity of experienced female trainers. Vicki Vodon, a soft-spoken blonde who holds the unlikely title of women's world arm-wrestling champion, began studying to be an athletic trainer when she was a student at California State College in Los Angeles. When the women athletes had injuries, they had to trek over to the men's side of the gym, since all of the trainers were male. "The trainer always had one cure for a woman," says Vicki. "He said, 'Go take aspirin.' " Sometimes 'Go take aspirin' is a reasonable treatment, but Vicki was upset at the arrogance and indifference about women's bodies. Now, as the women's trainer at the University of California, Los Angeles, Vicki dispenses whirlpool treatments and massages, as well as tape for sprained ankles. "A lot of trainers don't believe in massages," she says, "but I'm trying to get women in touch with their own bodies, so they understand what they're feeling. Most women don't know their bodies, so when something goes wrong they get worried and rely on someone else to cure them."

When strains or aches flare up—as they will, notably at the beginning of a new exercise program—standard homespun remedies can sometimes be harmful. For example, it's not true that a long soak in a hot tub makes everything feel better after sports. In fact, hot water can turn a simple sprain into a major disaster. When heat is applied too soon to an injury, blood rushes into the area and causes swelling. Cold compresses should be applied to all strains or sprains for twenty-four hours, or until all signs of swelling have disappeared. An ice pack will constrict blood vessels and minimize swelling and pain—which is why a baseball pitcher "ices" his arm after a game, sometimes for several hours. Dr. John Marshall recommends "R.I.C.E." for most pains and injuries—rest, ice, compression, and elevation. When you come home from any activity that involves pounding on your legs—running on concrete, basketball, or field hockey, for example—hop into a warm shower if you must (tepid is better), but make sure you finish by splashing cold water on the calves for at least a minute or two. Since I've been recommending this plan to my active friends, they report fewer leg pains and less swelling at the ankles. One high school gym teacher tells me that she's always reminding her students that cold is better than hot for their bruises and strains, but the advice isn't heeded. "Most girls would be a lot better off," she says, "if we could get rid of the oversolicitous mothers with their hot soaks and Epsom salts. The best cure for mild pains? Ignore them."

The female body isn't easily harmed. It can survive basketball as well as childbirth, rugby in addition to mothering. If male and female children were raised under similar conditions, it's likely that some gap would still exist between men's and women's sports abilities—though exactly how narrow that gap would be is hard to say. Right now women's limitations in sports have less to do with genetics than with the social codes that keep women alienated from their bodies.

Chapter Three

Femininity and Feminism

For a woman to be independent means she can't be a woman,
she must be a dyke. That in itself should tell us where women are at.
It says as clearly as can be said: woman and person are contradictory terms.
—Radicalesbians

If sports novelist Zan Knudson had been writing her children's books when I was growing up, I might have become a jock instead of a writer. But the sports books I read were always aimed at boys, and calling a girl a jock was condemning her to purgatory. Some women athletes still struggle with the connotations of their role and seek questionable means of absolution. One afternoon before an important track meet in California, Zan watched some female runners warming up; as they jogged and stretched and psyched themselves for the starting gun, there were whispered predictions that some records might be broken by the end of the day. With a novelist's eye for detail, Zan began noticing the number of runners on the track wearing jewelry, and she spotted one of her favorites wearing an ankle bracelet, earrings, two rings, and a necklace. "I was disgusted," she says. "I went up to her and said, 'Don't you know that Roger Bannister shaved an ounce off the sole of his sneakers before he broke the four-minute mile? He thought an extra ounce might make the difference, and here you've got four ounces of gold hanging around your body. What's the point?' "

The point is that away from storybooks even champions often have the uncomfortable feeling that something about their winning isn't quite right. The conflict over how to succeed without threatening one's femininity isn't limited to sports. In fact, it's so pervasive among women in all fields that schizoid tendencies have become routinized. Managerial consultants urge the female executive to pay for business lunches ahead of time, establish an account or join a club so that a male client doesn't have to confront having the check paid by a woman. Professional women are reminded that men will be less threatened by them if they wear a frilly blouse or gold necklace with their business clothes. "You learn a hundred tricks for dealing pleasantly with male subordinates," says one woman, "because the first time you slip and don't send out sugar with your orders you become known as The Bitch."

Right now the American woman is split—uncertain whether to be daddy's girl or Kate Millett's, she's trying to be both. The women who are involved in sports have trouble maintaining a dual facade. They know that for men, sports are often used as tests of machismo, ego-builders for the participants who require assurance of their power. The satisfaction which women derive from sports is often very different—fun, self-discovery, physical exhilaration. But because they're playing "male" games, women nervously wonder what having fun might say about their sexual identity. So women try to mask their raw power—with four ounces of gold jewelry or with denials. I've talked to women when they're still dripping with sweat from physical exertion and heard them disdainfully insist, "I'm not a feminist, you know." I always wonder what that means. That she's not a lesbian? That she wants to stay home with her children? That her husband supports her? Mostly the "I'm not a feminist" chant is a supplication for normality, an apology for having dared to step out of the fragile female role and be vigorous. The trouble so far in women's sports is that the athletes have been busy explaining, "I can do this *even though* I'm a woman," while few have been wise enough to claim, "This is *what it is* to be a woman." Obviously not all women athletes—in fact, very few of them—are motivated by feminist ideology.

Something more personal, like the pleasure of the activity itself or the good feeling it produces, has snared them; and those are better reasons to be in sports than a need to prove something, whether it's machismo or female power.

One woman who has accomplished an unapologetic mix of spirited independence and ladylike charm is Tenley Albright, who was the world ice-skating champion in the 1950s.[1] Tenley has always liked to set her own goals and then bound past them. She attended Radcliffe but dropped out after three years to practice seven hours a day for the 1956 Olympics. After winning the gold medal, she temporarily turned her back on skating to enter Harvard Medical School. Currently she is a surgeon in Boston, mother of three daughters, member of several skating and Olympic committees, and occasional athlete. "For a while I wanted to prove that I could do absolutely everything and not have any conflicts," she says. "I finally realized that it doesn't matter to my children whether I'm the one doing their laundry."

Growing up in a wealthy Boston family, Tenley was expected to be a socialite, not an athlete, and she had difficulty reconciling the two in the genteel fifties. Girls from Tenley's social class were expected to compete for boyfriends and husbands, and nothing else. "Every time I won something I would just hope that my picture didn't get put in the newspaper," she says. "My mother rationalized my competing to her friends by saying that I met nice people and got to take trips to Dubrovnik and Lucerne." Someone once introduced Tenley to me as "a super lady who's not even a feminist, not a liberated type at all." The gracious former champion just smiled, but it seemed a strange description for a woman who attended a largely male medical

1. In 1953, when she was seventeen, Tenley became the first American woman to win the world championship in figure skating. She repeated the win two years later, and also won two Olympic medals, including a gold in 1956. She never skated for money, but at the fiftieth anniversary of the United States Figure Skating Association, she appeared on a nationally televised show, skating a pairs routine with one of her three daughters, who was then six years old. "They wanted all the old-timers there, and we could either skate or be pulled out on a sled," says Tenley. "It wasn't a choice."

school and leaped around the world collecting trophies. "All that means," she said later, "is that I've accepted who I am. Things have gone well enough so I haven't had to become militant and I don't go searching for labels." She's proof that debutantes can be athletic and jocks can be smart. Tenley in some ways credits her skating experience with giving her the nerve to pursue medicine. When she applied to Harvard, she was sent to meet a female doctor who was sufficiently gruff and androgynous to send any young woman scurrying to nursing school, sure that a medical school degree just wasn't worth the sacrifice. "But I had already been an athlete," laughs Tenley, "and I knew that you couldn't get much worse than that."

Newspaper reporters loved following Tenley on her skating tours: They called her "apple-cheeked" and "pert and pretty" and kept careful watch on who kissed her after each competition. As the darling of the press, she ushered in the era of figure skater as American sweetheart. A decade after Tenley's triumphs, skating was just about the only sport in which a woman could hope to make any money, and that was because the ice shows were always looking for pretty girls who could stand up on skates. Champions learned that gold bred gold, and skaters like Peggy Fleming and Janet Lynn and Dorothy Hamill turned their Olympic medals into big-money contracts with the Ice Capades and Ice Follies. But for most, the jobs were inordinately disillusioning. Girls who ended up in the chorus lines of the shows spent more time being fitted for costumes than they did skating, and many abandoned the shows in bitterness. The thrill of amateur competition was gone, and only the backstage backbiting remained. "I'd been skating since I was five," says one girl, "and I dreamed of being a great star, a great athlete. But after dragging around with the ice show for a while, I quit. They put us in costumes that made me feel more like a call girl than a skater. I was sad for a while after I left and wondered why there isn't some way that a girl can be respected for the way she uses her body without sexing it up. Why do we have to be spectacles for people to gawk at?"

Skill has its place in skating, but ultimately image is everything. After Hamill abdicated the world figure-skating throne to become a million-dollar pro, it was time to find the next young innocent who could become an ice queen. A dark-haired Italian-American from Northridge, California, Linda Fratianne, qualified. Possibly the first American skating star with a non-WASP name, she captured her first national championship in 1977 with a performance so exciting that when the lights dimmed because of a power shortage, the word went around that this bright young skater had blown the fuses. Four weeks later she captured the world figure-skating title. Her coach, Frank Carroll, told me shortly afterward that Linda was an all-around superb skater with technical expertise, incredible tricks (including triple jumps), and balletic fluidity. But he was worried. "She needs to improve the performance value of her program," he said. "I want her to give more to the audience." During the next year, Linda worked with a drama coach on how to love an audience and offer kisses, gestures, and smiles. Carroll began picking Linda's clothes and teaching her how to talk to reporters and fans. But although Carroll helped Linda become a champion, he couldn't quite make her a star, and the next year she finished second in the world championships. Athletic excellence wasn't enough.

Similarly, at the 1976 Winter Olympics, many people thought that speed skater Sheila Young would emerge as the full-blown media star. She won more medals than Dorothy Hamill, but ultimately, Sheila was like the winning car at the Indy 500—a vehicle to be admired, not loved. Wearing a dark blue uniform which covered every inch of flesh, Sheila depended solely on strength and skill for her victories, not sensuality. Americans have trouble with female athletes who are invulnerable, too competent, too unneeding of affection.

Figure skaters entice the imagination by wearing sequined dresses, flesh-colored tights, and charming smiles. They glide to pretty music, twirling so fast that their panties show. They are our ruddy-cheeked girls of winter: slightly spoiled, very graceful, all-American dreams. Even Portnoy found his first snub-nosed girl friend at the edge of an ice rink. The skating world demands that its champions be prettily groomed and mannered and rewards them generously for being so. When Janet Lynn signed her contract with the Ice Follies to become the highest-paid woman athlete in the country, she hadn't even won a world championship. But Jim McKay, a broadcaster for ABC-TV's "Wide World of Sports," had fallen in love with her alluring smile and promoted her into a national heroine. One later champion described her as "an angel reaching toward God." This successor continues, "Janet added less to the sport in terms of technique or athletic style than any other national champion, but she was every father's dream girl, and people wanted her to win so they could hug her."

Girls who move up through the competitive ranks learn to pay as much attention to their costumes as to their figure eights. Dorothy Hamill admitted that cultivating a Goody Two-Skates image helped her in the sport; and one very talented skater was advised by officials of the U.S. Figure Skating Federation that she'd never start collecting medals if she continued to be out-spoken and critical of authorities. Linda Fratianne now under-stands that power and skill aren't enough. So she wakes up at 4:00 every morning to spend an hour putting on base, rouge, mascara, eye shadow, and lip gloss before going to the ice rink. Her concern with feminine accoutrements almost spoiled rather than saved her career. One week before a championship she was practicing a Russian split jump and caught her skate on a ring she was wearing. The ensuing fall left her with a torn inner-thigh muscle. "I'm a little more careful about jewelry now," she says. She still takes a blow dryer to her hair about three times a day to prevent the frizzies and insists that "every-one would die" if they saw her looking natural.

The amateurs must be charming and innocent, but when they sign up for the ice shows they must change all that. When Dorothy Hamill became the golden queen of the Ice Capades she was a slightly naive teenager who had done nothing but skate her whole life and still traveled with a rag doll for companionship. The wardrobe director was having none of that. At Hamill's first fitting, she found that her elaborate costumes came complete with grossly padded bras. Dorothy raged against looking like a burlesque star with silicone injections, but nowhere in her contract was she given the right to pull the stuffing out of her costumes. "Audiences don't want great skating from a girl," says one Ice Capades insider. "They want color and sex and entertainment. Dorothy would like to just go out and skate, I suppose, but she's got to understand that nobody is ready for that."

Women's advances in sports proceeded at a typically modest rate until 1972 when Congress passed the Educational Amendments Act. Title IX of the law prohibited a school from receiving federal funds if it displayed any form of sex discrimination. The members of the Department of Health, Education, and Welfare who drafted the law understood that it would have a volcanic effect on women's sports, the one area where sexual discrimination was still rampant in most schools. ("Boys were allowed into cooking classes long before Title IX," said one official.) At the junior high school I attended, our huge gym had a partition in the middle to separate it into boys' and girls' areas. I always assumed that someone had miscalculated where the middle was, since the boys had about three times as much space as we did. That was the least of the inequities that Title IX was intended to remedy. American universities were generally allocating less than one percent of their total athletic budgets to women's activities, and there probably wasn't a high school or elementary school in the country that offered boys and girls equal opportunities in sports. Big schools like the University of Nebraska or Ohio State were working with athletic budgets of three or four million dollars. Maybe half a million dollars went to the football team—understandable since that's what produced most of the revenue—while the women were tossed about $10,000 total for all their teams. It's true that a women's field hockey team doesn't require the same monstrous budget as a Big Ten football team, and Title IX didn't demand that schools give the new women's teams the ridiculous luxuries that the men were afforded. What was expected was some spirit of equality. Maybe the women didn't need two-and-a-half-pound steaks as training meals, but if the men had a few million dollars to play with, couldn't the women at least have enough money to stop at McDonald's after a game? Athletic directors around the country shook their heads. The administrators of four private universities in Washington, D.C., bought a full-page newspaper ad to proclaim their Declaration of Independence. Their top-level explanation was that they didn't want governmental interference with their institutions—but it's interesting that they chose this case to assert a philosophical right. Essentially, it seemed that they had decided it would be better to refuse federal funds than to give women a fair chance in sports.

The governing body for men's college sports, the National Collegiate Athletic Association (NCAA), banned women until 1974 and spent almost $300,000 lobbying against Title IX. Officials made dramatic statements auguring the demise of men's sports if women were given any share of the athletic budgets. They maintained such piety about the evils of robbing Peter to pay Pauline that some wondered if the morality of women's sports had been decided in the Bible. But, as the old story goes, reports of the death of men's sports were greatly exaggerated, and information on how quickly women's budgets were growing turned out to be deceptive. "Sure our budget is twenty times bigger than it was last year," snapped the women's swimming coach at a small college, "but have you stopped to think exactly what twenty times zero equals?" At the University of California, Berkeley, administrators announced one fall that expenditures on women's sports had been boosted by 1000 percent over the year before. That seemed wildly exorbitant and had NCAA officials clutching their chests and moaning again—until someone pointed out that women were still receiving only 2 percent of the school's total athletic expenditures.

From an alphabet soup of confusion, the Association for Intercollegiate Athletics for Women (AIAW) gradually emerged as the women's equivalent of the NCAA.[2] It was the first governing body in women's sports that could enforce policy. Previously, most women's athletics had been under governmental auspices. "The international scene of the nineteen fifties and sixties had put pressure on the government to take women's college sports more seriously," says Phyllis Bailey, the gray-haired assistant director of athletics at Ohio State and the only woman involved in allocating that school's multimillion-dollar athletic budget. "The Olympics had become a political battlefield, and our men were getting medals but our women weren't. We had to do something to protect our standing in the world and get American women on a par with others. Most of us wanted the changes to come from within the educational mainstream."

Nearly three hundred schools joined the AIAW as charter members, and it soon became evident that women's sports were growing so quickly that they would soon be revenue-producing. That phrase rang bells at the NCAA; in 1975, the men began a frenzied effort to gain control of women's sports. "The whole thing smacks of the neighborhood bully coming down the block," claimed Marge Polivy, the AIAW attorney at the time. With their own organization developing nicely, the women had no interest in submitting to patriarchal rule, and they set up great lobbying efforts of telephone calls, letter-writing, and speech-making to preserve their autonomy. The men arrogantly abandoned the prospectus for a joint organization when it became clear the women wouldn't join the hierar-

2. The history of the women's sports organizations is convoluted. Regulations were initially set by the Division of Girls' and Women's Sports (DGWS), a part of the American Alliance for Health, Physical Education and Recreation (AAH-PER). That group changed its name to the National Association for Girls' and Women's Sports (NAGWS), which spawned the Commission on Intercollegiate Athletics for Women (CIAW)—replaced in 1971 by the AIAW.

chy as tokens; they insisted on being treated as equals. Some, like Phyllis Bailey, who had been involved with the transitions in women's sports since the mid-1950s, could never forget the wrongful treatment that women had received before. "Life back then was incredibly frustrating for any woman who cared about sports," she says. "All those false barriers about what was and wasn't suitable for us. I suppose the driving force in my life ever since has been to make sure that other women don't suffer the same frustration and confusion that I did."

Bailey, a tall woman with a wry sense of humor, always considered herself a jock, not a feminist, and for a long time avoided most women's action groups. "But one day it hit me in the face that whether I liked it or not, I couldn't run away from the women's rights issues," she says. "Women have the chance to be in the driver's seat, and we'd better take it, no matter what that involves. When this job was first offered to me, I didn't know if I should accept because it involved constantly standing up for the woman's position against three or four men. I didn't like the idea of being that aggressive. But men are used to keeping things under their control, and they'll keep it that way until there are women who won't back away from them." Bailey sometimes seems surprised by her own strength, but she wields it with quiet dignity. Her anxiety over being an "aggressor" is surprisingly common among athletic women, who often are tigers on the field and pussycats off it. Since sports demand that they be strong-minded but traditional expectations demand otherwise, conflicts arise no matter what they do.

Buck Dawson, the director of the Swimming Hall of Fame, says that the history of female liberation can be traced through the swimsuits that women have worn. It's probably true—they reveal the proscriptions and social manacles that women athletes have endured. The women have been painfully passive, wearing whatever the men in charge expected or demanded. Back at the turn of the century, the only acceptable bathing garb covered just about every inch of the female body. Men insisted that swimming was too rigorous for women and that they would drown if they ventured into water beyond wading depth. Their prophecy was sometimes confirmed—not because women were too weak to swim, but because they were pulled under by the yards and yards of heavy wet material. When the Amateur Athletic Union decided in 1915 to let women swim competitively—if you can call it that—for the first time, they were permitted to wear knee-length suits, as long as they were made of thick black wool. A few angry women tried to shed the dead weight, but they didn't receive much sympathy. Restrictions on public swimming attire were even more severe. An Olympic champ named Ethelda Bleibtrey was arrested for "nude bathing" on a New York beach when she appeared without the stockings that were then required.

All this history is worth more than a belly laugh, though, because it points to women's lack of control over their physical selves. And, unbelievably, it wasn't until long after Steinem and Millet and others had begun expounding women's right to freedom, physical freedom, that American swimmers shed their impedimenta and put on streamlined suits. The change came in 1973, when the East Germans, logically willing to damn modesty for the sake of victory, appeared at the World Games wearing tight-fitting Lycra suits without skirts. The incident caused an enormous ruckus because until then the American women had been required to wear suits with small skirts in the front. Even after the East Germans dramatically defeated the Americans, the Amateur Athletic Union was reluctant to remove the brakes from its primly attired women. "It seems incredible because the stupidity of that rule was so obvious," says Debbie Meyer, who won three gold medals in swimming in the 1968 Olympics. "I'm convinced that I could have gone a couple of seconds faster if we'd been allowed to wear those suits when I was competing. After 'seventy-three, a couple of girls got the Lycra suits and sewed a little frilly lace on the bottom so they'd have a skirt. The AAU finally changed the rule. But could it be that officials honestly believed people would come to swim meets just to look at a swimmer's crotch?"

Trying to come to grips with such attitudes and with herself sent Debbie into a shock spiral when she retired from competitive swimming at twenty, more than three years after her Olympic triumph. She had spent most of her life working to become a champ, and she was used to dividing the world into swimmers and nonswimmers rather than boys and girls. Her coach, Sherm Chavoor, recognized Debbie's potential early and developed an extremely close and protective relationship with her. While her high school classmates in Sacramento, California, worried about boyfriends and fraternity pins, Meyer thought about getting to bed by nine o'clock in order to be rested for her early-morning workouts. "The only time I dated was in groups with other swimmers who Sherm approved," she says, "and he let all the guys know that the rule was hands off Debbie. I didn't mind because everything I had was focused on swimming." The one-track existence freed her from all real-world dilemmas, and the fairy-tale life paid off with dozens of medals, broken records, and awards. Chavoor understood that in the highest echelons of competition, where stars are made on tenths of seconds, the slightest mental quirk can result in defeat. Shielding his prodigy from the uncertainties of being a female athlete in a male world was vital. She accepted him as a father-protector, allowing him, in effect, to run her life and assume all responsibility for her "nonfemale" competitive behavior. While she was swimming, Debbie was totally free from the conflicts that other young women swimmers often feel. She had a strong sense of herself as an athlete, a good athlete, and that was enough.

It wasn't enough, though, when she finally left swimming. All at once the real world seemed more chilling than any frost-covered swimming pool. "I didn't know what to do with myself and couldn't figure out where I fit in," she says. "I didn't know what people who weren't swimmers were expected to be like." How to make the transition from athlete to woman when suddenly faced with the unsuspected fact that people often assumed that the two terms were contradictory? "I was scared that I didn't know how to be a normal female. At first I figured the thing to do was not exercise at all. My muscles atrophied and I got horribly fat. I kept eating and not exercising and getting more and more depressed." The 6000 calories per day which she had needed to sustain her swimming workouts didn't cheer her, and for the first time in her life, Debbie was at odds with her body. "She had broken her ankle skiing at Lake Tahoe," says her mother, "and all she did was stay home and hobble back and forth to the refrigerator." In a few months she ballooned from her competitive weight of 130 pounds (on a 5'9" frame) to 180. Her once firm and perfectly conditioned body was oozing with fat, and she seemed to be trying to obliterate everything that she had once been. She left northern California and transferred to UCLA in the fall of 1972, but the move didn't provide much diversion from the circle of self-hate she was building. "Everyone there was so body-conscious that if you wanted to be looked at as a girl you had to be slim. I got very introverted, hid in my room, and wouldn't talk to anybody." Her mother sent her to a doctor and she lost twenty pounds—then gained them back with interest. Everything fell apart. The CBS officials who had hired her to do occasional commentary on the "Sports Spectacular" show eased her out, feeling that she was too heavy to appear on camera. They couldn't promote her as either jock or woman—she was just an indeterminate blob.

That did it. If the only way to function as a woman in the nonsports world was to get skinny, she would. With the same determination she had called on to become a champion, she put herself on a diet of about 500 calories a day: a little chicken with curry powder, a quarter-cup of rice, some vegetables, and a taste of fruit. She stuck with it until she was down to 108 pounds and was so delighted at being skinny that she didn't even care about the total collapse of her strength. Though once accustomed to swimming ten miles a day, Debbie passed several days in which she hardly had enough energy to get out of a bathtub. But she was so proud of her accomplishment that she went to visit her parents, who had moved to the Philippines. "My mother hadn't seen me in a while, and she took one look at me and was on the phone to the doctor. The next morning I was in his office. He diagnosed anorexia nervosa, low potassium, urinary-tract problems, low blood pressure, anemia, and broken capillaries."

Anorexia is almost exclusively a woman's disease, generally restricted to women under twenty-five who are so eager to have admirable and feminine figures that they lose all sense of what their bodies should look like and diet until their health is endangered. In a letter to *MS. Magazine* that appeared in December, 1976, two female therapists at Cornell University wrote that they had found anorexia nervosa to be caused by "the cultural factors that socialize women to be compliant and passive, and to value their bodies not for what they do or feel, but for how slim they are." Debbie was a fine example. "My life had fallen apart," she says. "After I quit swimming I thought of myself as a freak and sat around having an existential crisis. I finally just crawled into bed and let my mother take care of me and coax my weight back to a reasonable level." Within a few months, Debbie realized something surprising: She missed her muscles and she missed having a healthy feeling in her body. "It occurred to me that I love sports and that there was really no reason to stay away from swimming. Being like all the other girls is actually very boring." So her story had a happy ending, and she was hired as the assistant swim coach at Stanford. "It was time to take responsibility for my own life and not depend on Sherm," she says. "It had taken a while, but I finally felt like I was all grown up."

Debbie was an inspiring image to the women on the Stanford team. "You don't normally think of women as being authority figures," said one of her charges, "and at first I didn't trust Debbie at all. But it turned out great to have her there. Some cold mornings I'd come out and think, I can't do this, I'm just a girl. Then I'd see Debbie standing there and I'd know that if she'd managed, I could, too." Because they were socialized to believe that the athletic body is the antithesis of the female one, these women are constantly torn: As long as they're in sports they want to do well, but when they do, they wonder if there's something wrong with them. So their self-perception becomes confused, and they fluctuate wildly between a desire to be frail and delicate, and the realization that being so makes them feel despicable. "Debbie understood those splits," says Jo Harshbarger, who was one of the team members. "When we began to talk I couldn't believe how much we had in common. I don't think I would have lasted without her example."[3]

Jo was fifteen years old and a sophomore in high school when she competed in the 1972 Olympics. She had been swimming competitively for ten years and was thoroughly caught up in her sport, but she still hated the idea of people looking at her in a bathing suit. Unlike Debbie, who had her conflicts with "normality" after she retired, Jo was already uncertain whether she wanted to be a typical high school girl or a swimmer. "I always had a hang-up about my body," says Jo. "I thought I was too fat and my shoulders were too broad and that I looked like a jock." Whether or not it matters, Jo looks decidedly unlike a jock, being a slim blonde with green eyes. "It wasn't as bad for me as for some girls because people were always telling me that I was pretty. But still I'd look in the mirror and think, Jo, you are so fat, you are really awful." Maybe all high school girls worry about that, but Jo had the added burden of knowing that she wasn't the same as all other high school girls: Her body was stronger. She was different.

Jo had set a world record in the 800-meter freestyle race in the Olympic trials, and if she had repeated her time in Munich, she would have won the gold medal. Before leaving for the Games, she told her parents that if she copped the gold, she was going to quit swimming forever. Instead, inexperience, nerves,

3. After a year of coaching at Stanford, Debbie left to become a full-time representative for Speedo swimsuits. Her salary at Stanford was $5400; the president of Speedo, Dale Aigner, offered her a lucrative contract with benefits that include travel and a company car. "I loved coaching," Debbie says, "but it was only reasonable that I leave."

and heaven-knows-what combined so that she came in sixth and returned home to daily workouts in a chilly pool. "Maybe if I had won, being a celebrity would have made it okay to be different," she says, "but this way I got home and realized that I just couldn't stand my body. So I went on a diet, and before I knew it, I was emaciated. I didn't have any muscles left. I remember my parents coming to watch me at a swim meet in Canada that winter, and when they saw me standing there in a bathing suit, it suddenly struck them how wasted I was. They told me that if I didn't start eating I'd not only keep losing in swimming, I'd probably die."

Jo recovered quickly from her mild case of anorexia nervosa, but the dilemma which led to the problem kept nagging. She joined her school band and became a cheerleader to remind herself that all was well, and she got a reassuring pat on the head when she was voted school homecoming queen. "It was absolutely the best thing that ever happened to me," she says. "I was shocked because I figured everybody knew me as a swimmer, so they could never think of me as anything else. But they did." The final twist came when, after all her traumas and decisions, she didn't even qualify for the 1976 Olympics. "I would have quit swimming right after that, but I had an athletic scholarship to Stanford, which means I was pretty much being paid six thousand dollars a year to stay in the water. And there was Debbie, who made me realize that I didn't just have to be Jo the Jock. We have coed practices and I watch the guys, who are pretty laid back and just enjoy everything. That's what I'm trying to do now—think of swimming as just one of the things in my life. But I'm probably too fat again. I should lose five pounds."

The subliminal feeling of not really belonging in the activities they're pursuing leads many women to undermine their own sporting efforts. Debbie Meyer began to notice this when she was poolside at the Montreal Olympics and agitatedly watched the East German women grab eleven of thirteen gold medals. "Do you know why we lost? Because the U.S. women are ashamed to be athletes and the East Germans aren't. Our women were a disgrace—not because they didn't win all the gold, that's no tragedy, but because they pretended that it really wasn't important to be good. They said some awfully immature things, and I just wanted to go over and shake them."

The comments which appalled Debbie were largely attributed to Shirley Babashoff, a nineteen-year-old American star whose championship quest was blocked by the stronger East Germans. Shirley wasn't exactly a failure in the Games, since she won four silver medals and a gold, but she was bitter about consistently finishing an eyelash behind her East German nemesis, Kornelia Ender, who emerged as the undisputed heroine of the meet.[4] Shirley saw herself as loser, and she was a sore loser at that—her hometown newspaper, the *Los Angeles Times*, dubbed her "surly Shirley." When asked to comment on the East Germans' success, Shirley just tossed her head and sniffed, "Who wants to be like them, anyhow?" The sour-grapes reaction was unbecoming, since presumably Shirley would have given a good deal to be a winner like Kornelia; that's why she was in Montreal, right? But once again a female identity crisis had overruled logic. "She doesn't want to be stereotyped as a jock, and she's actually psyching herself out that way," said Debbie Meyer. Having received widespread publicity for her swimming feats for years, Shirley was worried about her image. Since swimmers generally keep their hair short to be practical, Shirley grew hers very long and made fun of the other women's "butch" look. At the Olympics, she targeted her snipes at the broad-shouldered East Germans, hinting they had become the best in the world by being more man than woman.

She wasn't the only one with that gripe. Ever since the East German women had grabbed the title of international swim champs from the Americans in 1973, there had been sugges-

4. Shirley dropped out of the finals of one race to give herself a better chance at winning in her specialty, the 800-meter freestyle. Kornelia stayed in both races. She won the first, disappeared to change bathing suits, and came back twenty minutes later to beat Shirley in the 800. It was the first time anyone won two gold medals in a half hour.

tions that they took male hormones and steroids to increase their muscle size. At the Olympics, one broadcaster asked an East German trainer why so many of the women had deep voices. He looked surprised. "They have come here to swim, not to sing. Why do you concern yourself with their voices?" The accusations might have had some validity, but there was also an element of subterfuge. "Our women lose because they're afraid to be tough," says one American male coach. "The East Germans start pushing weights when they're eight years old, but we don't bother with that. We don't expect much from our women, so we don't get it." Shirley's attempts to vindicate herself by calling on her femininity also rang hollow since Kornelia Ender was an unmistakably pretty eighteen-year-old and the fiancée of Roland Matthes, a swimmer on the East German men's team. Before every race, she demurely handed her engagement ring to a judge for safekeeping.

Often women's athletics are accepted only when sporting attitudes have become mixed with traditionally feminine ones. One example of this is in Iowa, where girls' high school basketball is as much of a staple as wheat. Basketball season starts in the middle of November, and after the regular games end in February the qualifying tournaments begin: sectional play-offs, districts, and regionals. The sixteen surviving teams are invited to the state tournament in Des Moines, and when the girls arrive, the city is festooned with banners welcoming the "Sweet Sixteen." Wherever the girls go there is hoopla: Bands play, fans cheer, and the governor appears and gives someone or other an award. A week or so later the boys' tournament is usually held, but the city doesn't dazzle quite so much for that, and the auditorium is never as packed.

During the week of the girls' championships, many of the smaller towns in the state virtually close down as parents and fans pack into trailers to follow the girls. Of the 503 high schools in the state, 494 have a girls' basketball team. There are never enough seats in Veterans Auditorium for everyone who wants them. Over 100,000 paying fans pass through the turnstiles, and several television stations preempt their regular programming to broadcast the girls' games live. The first championship game was played in the state in 1919, and since then the fresh-faced Iowa girls have played an old-fashioned game in which there are six players on a side instead of five, not much dribbling, and almost no running. The man who runs basketball in Iowa is Wayne Cooley, who has been in charge of girls' sports in the state since the 1950s. One tradition he accepts is that the men control everything. "We don't need women coaches or women administrators to make this program work," he says. "If I hired some, they'd probably have babies in a year or two and quit, and we'd just have to start again." Because he was an advocate of girls' basketball long before anyone else, Cooley resents it when outsiders suggest that his program is mired in male chauvinism. "I was a nigger to people for a long time because I believed in girls," he says. "Other people are catching up now, but why should I listen to them?"

The antiquated six-on-a-side girls' rules have been widely denounced, but Cooley is willing to fight for them. "My young ladies aren't strong enough to play by standard rules," he says. "Besides, watching the girls play this way isn't threatening to the male spectators, it's amusing." In Tennessee, a fifteen-year-old girl argued in court that playing the girls' rules (which her state also used) limited her chance for getting an athletic scholarship to college. When she won, Cooley claimed that feminist forces from the East had set up the Tennessee case and would be gunning for him next. He had lawyers prepare legal briefs, but it was a while before anyone sued—possibly because the Iowa girls are so indoctrinated to his system. "Playing by boys' rules wouldn't be right," says one girl from Lake View–Auburn Community School, which boasts the most successful team in the state. "Why should we? Our coach says that the main reason we play basketball is to get poise and grace and become better ladies."

The girls from Lake View–Auburn don't understand much about feminism and they don't understand about discrimination. They play basketball because it's the most exciting thing to do in Lake View, population: 1200. The nearest movie theater is thirty miles away and the nearest shopping center is twenty miles away. After school a girl can either work in the cornfields or play basketball. Both are acceptable activities, but with basketball there's a chance of winning the trip to Des Moines, with the incumbent week-long shopping spree. And for many of the girls, basketball is the only chance they'll ever have to shine—not many go on to college and even fewer continue with athletic careers. When the Lake View girls lost in the semifinals one year, a senior on the team was inconsolable. "This is the one time in my life when I could have been special," she confided to me tearfully, "and I'll never have a chance like it again. Now I go back to being a nonentity."

The Lake View coach is Bud McCrea, a tall, fair-haired Scotch-Irishman who is hailed as a genius throughout the state for his coaching triumphs, which have included two consecutive championships. On the court, his girls have license to be aggressive and uninhibited—an indulgence rescinded immediately after the final whistle. Walking toward the locker room, Bud reminds the girls that "a lady is above opening doors for herself." He repeats such sentiments so often that one half-expects him to change the name of his basketball summer camps to McCrea Charm School, Inc. "I usually think of girls as broads or chicks," he says to me, "but the ones who play basketball for me have to become ladies. That means something special, because you have to like yourself and be proud of what you do before you can be a lady." McCrea is also principal at Lake View–Auburn, but that is a secondary obligation; it's planning basketball strategy that keeps him awake nights. "What sets my girls apart is their attitude," he says. "This game is about seventy percent mental, and I'll do anything to give a player confidence." His word is gospel, but to keep spirits buoyed even more, the local reverend, a liberal, joking minister named Dick Viney, travels to the championships with the team. He slips into the locker room before games and has the girls join hands in a unity prayer. He makes it clear that if Bud McCrea is not exactly God, he is at least the king. "There are no stars among the players because Bud is the only leader," he says. "He is the man, and the girls are his followers."

Every year during States there is a reunion for members of past championship teams, and over a hundred women arrive—most now farmers' wives and secretaries—to relive their moments of fame. Dressed in their self-conscious best, they listen with small smiles as Cooley reminds them of their rendezvous with immortality. "Iowa does not forget," he intones. "You are the finest women in the state."

"We use basketball in this state to develop ladies who will be respected by their menfolk and willing to work hard," says one gray-haired matron. Another agrees. "We don't believe in women's lib here. We were all just small-town girls who had a chance to hear applause once in our lives. I guess you could say we reached our pinnacle at age sixteen."

If something has gone wrong for the Iowa women it may be that they have been used as sporting playthings, enticed by the pleasures of their activity but never allowed to grow with it. For Wayne Cooley, girls' basketball is entertainment. He embellishes the half-time show with acts like the Dubuque Golden Girls, who wear tight skirts and high boots and wiggle for whistles. "We put on the best entertainment show in the state," he says. "It doesn't matter if the game's lousy because there's so much color and excitement surrounding it. People used to say that I was prostituting the girl athletes by selling admissions, but that's not true. The spectators are genuinely interested in the girls." He pauses when asked why that might be, catching the insinuation behind the question. "If you accused the men of Iowa of being girl-watchers, I think they'd be very upset," he says. One wonders if the women are similarly upset at finding that sports are a short-lived dream, an introduction to unconstrained possibility which must end when womanhood begins.

Is there a chance for change in this situation? Probably. It's generally true that when defenselessness and vulnerability are accepted traits for women, athletic prowess is not—but in Iowa, these conflicting postures exist in an uneasy alliance. One way to change attitudes is to change behavior first, and that is certainly occurring. Basketball is no longer the only important girls' sport in Iowa—there are now state championships in several other sports, including track and field and gymnastics. Boys and girls in schools in Cedar Rapids share virtually equal access to good coaching and equipment. Once everyone is out playing, girls worry less about hiding their skills. Gradually, being a winner becomes part of the definition of being a woman.

Chapter Four

Sex and Sports

The voice of the sea is seductive; never ceasing, whispering, clamoring, murmuring, inviting the soul to wander for a spell in abysses of solitude; to lose itself in mazes of inward contemplation. The voice of the sea is sensuous, enfolding the body in its soft, close embrace.
—*Kate Chopin*

The Muriel Grossfeld Gymnastics School in Connecticut is one of the best in the country. It is run by a dynamic former champion who once gave up a Hollywood career to pursue her interest in sports. Despite her reputation for being a tyrant, Muriel has been known to hug and comfort her charges even when they lose. At the school, on eight acres of land that was once an apple orchard, about a dozen top gymnasts aged eleven to eighteen live year round in a remodeled colonial house next door to the Grossfeld gymnasium. During the school year they take classes at Milford Academy and are excused by 1:00 P.M. so that they can go to the gym and train for six or seven hours. The teen and preteen gymnasts generally appear for their daily workouts in colorful leotards, topped by T-shirts with slogans like LOVE A GYMNAST or GYMNASTS MAKE BETTER LOVERS. The girls are both too young and too busy training to take the slogans seriously, and they just giggle when asked about them. But there are many athletes who insist that the girls are on the right track, and there really is a connection between sports participation and female sexuality. "I wouldn't doubt it," says one young champ who has been training with Grossfeld for several years.

"There's so much physical joy in gymnastics. Isn't that what sex is kind of about?"

Physiologically, it's hard to prove that sports increase sexual energy, but the anecdotes from athletes are convincing. Probably more than anything else, an athlete's ease in her own body and understanding of her physical self encourage sensuality. "I'm much more sexually aggressive now because I've accepted myself and don't get embarrassed," says one woman. "I like my body because I like what my body can do. If a man rejects me, it's no big deal. I figure he doesn't know what he's missing." Skier Suzy Chaffee, who is utterly uninhibited about her own sexuality, has a similar attitude. "Love is a bummer if it's based on fear of survival—if he has all the money, power, and confidence and you don't have any," she says. "When you feel good about yourself you can play around in roles and be up-front about things. There's something very sexy about dealing with men from a basis of independence rather than need." Often sports can furnish this new, less vulnerable sense of self by offering women a new outlook that leads to sensual awakening.

One of the most beautiful novels written about a woman's self-discovery is Kate Chopin's classic *The Awakening*, daringly written in 1906. The heroine, Edna Pontellier, breaks away from her comfortable but too-restricted marriage during one glorious summer when she learns to swim. Chopin describes the venture as a symbolic and physical test of strength, connected with Edna's making the transformation from wife-mother to human being and taking a new lover: After years of sitting on the beach, Edna dares herself to challenge the waves. When she does, writes Chopin, "A feeling of exultation overtook her, as if some power of significant import had been given her to control the working of her body and soul. She grew daring and reckless. . . . She wanted to swim far out, where no woman had swum before." With this new understanding of her own power, a woman's sexual and spiritual sensibilities are aroused, and her life begins to change.

This transformation is more than a novelistic device; the

sensual delight of sports is very real. According to psychiatrist Dr. Robert Brown, participation in certain sports "is like having a thousand hands touching. There's new feeling in every part of your body." A Boston artist who runs year round says she feels sexually charged after she exercises. "There's something sexy about sweat," she says. "During the summer when it's really hot, I go three miles and end up collapsed by the reservoir, all sweaty and exhausted. My whole body is throbbing, and I'm not thinking about anything, just feeling. It's an incredible high." A woman who was captain of her prep school field hockey team many years ago says she and her teammates first encountered their sexual instincts on the field. "Guys on football teams always have a reputation for being studs, and it was the same with us," she says. "Everyone thinks that with the football players it's a macho thing, but it's not—it's a body thing. Our sport was a lot like football. You know, we'd be chasing up and down a field during practice, and that means your heart is pounding and your blood is flowing. You come inside afterwards and your body is tingling all over because you're so physically up and exhilarated. We'd sit around and talk about how horny we felt. Back then, none of the other women I knew would discuss things like that, but we were really charged."

Probably nobody ever misjudged the connections between sex and sports more than the headmasters of boys' private schools, who used to have the boys run around athletic fields to keep them from running after girls. The old notion of maintaining morality by cold showers and rough-and-tumble games probably stimulated boys (and later girls) more than it sated them. Helene Roberts of the Fogg Museum at Harvard University points out that one reason many Victorian ladies hated sex was that they were unacquainted with their own bodies. Accustomed to being bound by whalebone corsets and layers of hoops, crinoline, ruffles, and lace, they could scarcely move, let alone enjoy the feeling of their own bodies. Roberts suggests that when women's schools began putting games like basketball, cricket, and lacrosse into the curriculum in the 1890s, changes naturally followed. The girls couldn't participate unless they took off their restrictive clothing, and once they did that, the decorum of the Victorian era faced certain dissolution. Says Roberts: "The influence of sports in the 1890s was near revolutionary."[1] With corsets off, women began using the muscles that had previously been wasted; their bodies stopped seeming so inscrutable and they had an intimation that sex— just maybe—could be a nice activity instead of a terror. Sports like bicycling became the vogue along with bloomers as women began shedding physical and symbolic encumbrances. Elizabeth Cady Stanton, the well-known feminist of the period, reported: "Many a woman is riding to suffrage on a bicycle."

The loosening of strictures and the discovery of the body are still important aspects of sports, and the early feminists' breakthroughs are constantly being duplicated by average women. "I don't know why, but I'm a lot less uptight after I've been swimming or playing squash," says one woman who works out three times a week at a YWCA. "I don't get into as many petty fights with my husband." Another woman who frequents the same Y concurs. "It's not the sexist theory of exercising so you'll look better for 'him,' but it's feeling better about you. If you ask me, sexual prudery has nothing to do with morals—it's just that most women figure they look rotten with their clothes off and don't want anybody to see them."

One athlete who doesn't mind being seen is Jane Frederick, a 5'11" track and field star who has been the American champion in the pentathlon for years. The pentathlon is the women's equivalent of the decathlon, the event which usually determines the number-one all-around male athlete. Bruce Jenner made it to the Wheaties box by winning a gold medal in the event, and there's a good chance that after the next Olympics, Jane's picture will be next to Jenner's on every breakfast table. "I'm hooked on the physical pleasure of sports, and the fact that

1. Her study appeared in *Signs: Journal of Women in Culture and Society,* Vol. II, No. 3 (Spring 1977): 554.

participating has taught me to feel good about me," she says.

For my first interview with Jane, we had arranged to meet in front of the women's gym at UCLA. Since that's a popular spot, I mentioned what I'd be wearing and asked how I'd know her. "You'll know me," she said. I did. Built like a Greek goddess, she strides across campus with an easy carriage that commands attention. But it wasn't always that way. "I used to detest my body," says Jane. "I thought my shoulders were too wide, my legs were too long, and I was much too tall. I wore gops of makeup in high school because I wanted to cover me up. When you're not sure of yourself, everything is wrong—your eyelashes are never dark enough, your lips are never the right shape, your chin is too pointy, and your hair is impossible." She didn't fit in with the round and perky Annette Funicello look of the period, so the shy and gawky teenager joined a track club as an escape. A funny thing happened then: The more she achieved in track, the more she began to like herself. But it took several more years before she dared to stop hiding her body under bras and long-sleeved shirts. "One summer I was at a national meet in California, and I put on this little halter top because it was cool and I wanted to get a decent tan. Everybody started coming by and telling me how great I looked. All I could say was, 'Oh yeh? You *like* my shoulders? You mean they're not disgusting?' My self-image really changed after that, and people sensed it." Jane began collecting trophies and setting records at a remarkable rate. The trophies don't mean much to her—she keeps only one in her apartment and that doubles as a plant holder—but the real satisfaction came from her new buoyancy. "The pendulum has swung to the other side, and I'm wildly chauvinistic about myself," she grins. "I have very few inhibitions, and I can really respond physically. Men go cuckoo for me, they really do. I'm not afraid to be nude in front of anybody because I know that other people can enjoy me as much as I enjoy me. As long as I love my body, everybody else does, too."

If Jane's confidence threatens to spill over to narcissism, her forthright manner and grip on reality easily prevent that. "I've taught my body to do things, so of course I can have a great deal of faith in it," she says earnestly. "Women who don't do that are cheating themselves. I just wish every woman could look in the mirror and say, 'This is me, and it's just fine.'" But it sometimes seems that there's not another woman in the world able to do that. One successful fashion model I know told me that on her first visit to one of New York's formidable agencies, the director came in to grade her body, offering an A on hands, a B on breasts, and a C on thighs. For a week, the lovely model insists, she felt sexless and unattractive. "If I hadn't started getting some jobs I might have disappeared to a convent," she says. Matching themselves against some unattainable ideal, women frequent plastic surgeons and hair designers and makeup experts in efforts to make themselves feel better. But the satisfaction from such visits is fleeting. "I fall into this syndrome where I don't want men to get too close," says a public relations director for a San Francisco company. "That usually means that I've been doing all the right things on the outside, but I've been ignoring my body, so I feel out of shape, and basically rotten. How can I snuggle up with someone that way?"

The sexual attitudes of athletes vary from the refreshingly free and natural to the coarsely animalistic. "Athletes are so used to being body-oriented that sex is a natural part of their lives," says one Boston sportscaster. "I think they're healthier that way than most people." A much debated topic in many training rooms is whether sex before a game helps or hurts an athlete. Ken Norton, the heavyweight boxer, is adamant about sexual abstinence before a fight and says he harnesses his strength by sleeping alone. An easy opponent might merit six nights without women, while Muhammad Ali (whom Norton beat) was worth eight weeks. He admits that much of this is more important to mental preparation than to physical readiness. For some reason, more men than women seem to favor sexual continence before an important event—possibly because they associate sex with wild parties and heavy drinking, which can, indeed, take a toll. "Some men think that staying away from sex psychs them to win, but most of the women I know get psyched by having sex," says one professional freestyle skier. "When I started, someone told me that for freestyle you should be with your lover the night before so you look all secure and soft out there. But for downhill, you should reserve your strength. That's one of the most ridiculous things I've heard. You need to be loose in sports to do well, not all knotted up." Most people can regain their normal energy level three or four minutes after having an orgasm. Others may take a half hour. Unless you're unwittingly withdrawing from the intimacy, the only reason for falling asleep after an orgasm is because it's late and you're in bed for the night. Suzy Chaffee once insisted that she had sex every night during important competitions to release some of her volcanic energy. "Sports give you more energy for everything," she says, "and that includes energy to love and be tender with someone. I'm really into exchanging massages with a man, because that's a way to appreciate the total body and get through to the whole person. It's great reinforcement no matter what you're doing the next day." At a recent Super Bowl game, one coach announced that his players would be separated from their wives and girl friends the night before the event; the other coach decided that there would be no curfews and no restrictions on sleeping partners. The lovers won the game. Said one of the players afterward: "I don't think you win by screwing around, but you don't lose that way, either."

Many novice athletes find that sports give them a vibrancy that translates into sexual intensity. For example, one woman writer and fitness consultant from San Francisco, California, thinks sports are replacing bars as a way to meet people. "Wouldn't you rather meet the love of your life on a ski slope or at a marina than in a singles place? Sports lead to all kinds of socializing, and I want to be fit and ready any time a good, handsome, marvelous man wants to whisk me off to Aspen to ski. It works the other way, too, and I invite guys along all the time. If they don't ski as hard as I do and think they're saving themselves for the evening, forget it. I always flake out by eight o'clock." But she adds with a laugh: "I prefer sex in the morning because it gets you ready for the day."

A woman law student from Connecticut also insists on a connection between sex and sports. "Last winter I'd been spending all my time in the library," she says. "I'd gained about ten pounds, felt incredibly frumpy, and didn't want anybody even to touch me. I hadn't been running since Thanksgiving, but I pulled out a sweatsuit and started jogging through the snow every day. God, it felt good—like I was caring about myself again. About two weeks later I went to a discotheque and felt really slinky and desirable. The next morning I got on a scale and couldn't believe it, but I hadn't lost a pound the whole time. Maybe it didn't matter, because I'd regained possession of my body." A sampling of women at a New York racquet club reveals that the attitude is widespread. "Sensuality has more to do with how you feel than what you look like," explains one woman in her forties, "and when I've been banging a squash ball around, I feel powerfully alive. People can sense that." Another woman who has been playing and winning at corporate games recently began spending about two hours a week on the racquetball courts. "I'm very ambitious in my job and a lot of the men detest that," she says. "The word around the office used to be that I needed a good lay. Every afternoon I'd go into the ladies' room and cry, then come out more hard-assed than ever. Now I come here instead, and after a workout I feel so much better, so integrated, that any nasty comments about my sexuality just bounce off."

The men who live with or are married to athletic women speak about them in an almost reverential tone. Most recognize that these women have demanded something special from their own lives, so they have something extra to give. "There's a difference in the way an athletic woman feels and responds," says the husband of a gymnast. "I don't mean just my wife, but other women I've been with. Maybe my experience hasn't been that wide, but I'm convinced that they have an openness and pleasure in their bodies that makes them sexually powerful. She has a sexual energy that's awesome." Terry Todd, the husband of weight lifter Jan Todd, says that women who have learned to live with their bodies bring vigor and security to male-female relationships. "The classic idea is that the man is strong and the woman is weak," he says. "The man is the pillar holding up the house, and the woman is the vine gracing the trellis. But the clinging-vine image is singularly inappropriate for any woman interested in decency and self-acceptance. I see a beautiful body as one that has been achieved through work and will. A woman who creates a more muscular or powerful body for herself is in control of her life. To shun that is a social sickness. Think of our symbol of beauty: the *Playboy* image of large breasts and not a great deal else. A lot of men I know now have had their consciousnesses raised enough so that they think it no more beautiful to see a flaccid body on a woman than on a thoroughbred. Or think of it this way: If you've ever been hunting, you've seen a lion in the wild. It's muscular, exquisitely coordinated, and able to move well. Compare that to a caged lion in the zoo, which is a mere shell, a bare indication of the potential that lies within that tawny skin. To me, that's the difference between an athletic woman and the model-types that the fashion managers and social arbiters want us to accept."

When asked to name a "sexy" female athlete, most of the women in an informal sampling named the traditionally pretty stars like golfer Laura Baugh and skater Peggy Fleming, with a few votes for tennis player Evonne Goolagong. The men had different answers. One lanky accountant chose Russian basketball player Lasta Semenova. "Getting seven feet of woman with a very sweet face is the sexiest thing I can imagine," he said. Generally, the men surprised me by consistently selecting Billie Jean King, who was never mentioned by the women. "She's not beautiful," said one stockbroker, "but all that intensity and energy is incredibly attractive. You watch her standing on the baseline waiting for a ball and she just hums." Added another man: "I admire Billie Jean and I also think she's sexy. She doesn't throw sex at you, but you can sense her vibrations—and that's a lot more enticing than a low-cut dress."

Shortly after he began dating Chris Evert, actor Burt Reynolds claimed that women athletes are very sexy as long as they keep their vulnerability. When one circuit tennis player heard the comment, she shook her head. "Vulnerable isn't sexy. Vulnerable is weak, infantile, and regressive. Sorry, but I wouldn't give up one smidgen of independence for a date with Burt Reynolds." Still, Reynolds's reaction is understood in some circles, and when Chrissie was named as *Sports Illustrated* magazine's Athlete of the Year in 1977, the staff proceeded warily. For the cover picture, this sports champion was dressed in a replica of an 1884 tennis costume—a long white dress complete with bustle. The underlying message to male readers was that if they were dismayed at a woman's getting the magazine's highest honor, they could console themselves by looking at the picture of prim and proper Chris, standing straight-backed in an Edwardian setting of bentwood furniture and potted palms. Holding an outmoded tennis racket, she was hardly the image of an athlete to be reckoned with. The photograph suggested to male readers that while it was fashionable to recognize women as athletes, they could regard the whole thing as a joke.

Most vigorous women have become happily adept at ignoring the men who get intimidated by them. "Maybe some men are put off by me," says one champion volleyball player, "but those aren't the kinds of guys I want to hang around, anyway." Girls who were once taught that they'd never get anywhere by beating the boys have come to realize that the advice was bad. One male lawyer from Washington, D.C., who played several sports in college claims that he used to like women who admired his talents but couldn't equal them. He met his current lover, though, on a tennis court, where she beat him soundly. "She had great concentration and she didn't start making sweetheart sounds—you know, saying my shots were beautiful but just out, and her winners were luck. Maybe my ego's gotten stronger, but I was intrigued. For once having a woman *not* pander to me but just play with respect was seductive. At the end, we shook hands, and I knew I was going to keep coming back." If power is an aphrodisiac, it works equally well in either sex. "Winning gets your juices going," one woman says with a grin. "When I'm playing tennis with my boyfriend, he knows that if I don't win, he won't score." But for some, like a married woman in her late twenties, there's difficulty reconciling the old teachings with the new awareness. "Consciously, I always try to do my best," she says, "but subliminally I probably have trouble believing that it's all right to beat men. Last time I was home, I was playing billiards with my dad. He taught me how to play, and I know he's proud that I can do it well, but I just didn't want to beat him. I wouldn't say that I purposely goofed up, but my heart wasn't in trying too hard. Sometimes I wonder if I'm always being daddy's little girl when I play against a man."

Real-life little girls have been dominating the sports scene alarmingly, and the emphasis on youthful superstars may reflect the masculine anxiety over dealing with adult women on an equal basis. "If you're past puberty and athletic, men figure you'll castrate them," says a javelin thrower with some bitterness. "So they get excited over the prepubescents with nimble bodies who they can still fantasize about grabbing." Certainly a wave of young tennis players and gymnasts has captured the public imagination in recent years. Frank Bare, the president of the U.S. Gymnastics Federation, claims that his organization is encouraging very young girls into major competitions because they are the most adept at learning difficult maneuvers. But that is questionable, since the hardest tricks require strength, which comes with maturity.

For years, the outstanding gymnast in the world was Liudmila Turischeva, a dignified and beautifully muscled Russian woman who was still radiantly successful in her twenties. At the 1972 Olympics, Liudmila was the undeniable champion and won the gold medal for the best individual gymnast. But she was roundly ignored in the American media in favor of her teammate Olga Korbut, a frolicsome gymnast with a child's body. At the next Olympics, the elfin Olga was portrayed by television announcers as the old lady of the sport and was replaced by an even younger star, fourteen-year-old Nadia Comaneci of Romania. Not long afterward, Nadia passed through a normal growing-up phase, and she arrived for a tour of America a few inches taller and many pounds heavier. Her flippy ponytail had been cut off, womanly hips were beginning to emerge, and much of her gleeful childishness was gone. From the negative reviews after her arrival, it's clear that no matter how much Nadia improves now as a gymnast, some of her male followers will feel forever betrayed that someone they admired as an athlete has dared to turn into a woman.

Men should know better, since a more than fair share of (grown-up) American sex symbols have been former athletes. Hollywood queen Esther Williams made her movie extravaganzas only after earning recognition as a swimming champion. She qualified for the 1940 Olympics, but the Games were canceled when World War II broke out. "I was heartbroken," she said many years later, "but I guess it's not worth regretting. I made a lot more money being a sex symbol than I would have as a gold medal winner." Movie impresarios in the forties and fifties found as many would-be stars on sports fields as in malt shops. A scout from Metro-Goldwyn-Mayer discovered "blonde and shapely" Kay Rohrer one day when she was playing softball in California. They offered her a contract and eventually promoted her as the "Softball Siren." Harpo Marx once joked that she was the only first baseman he ever wanted to kiss, but Kay left Hollywood and returned to softball before he could try. Apparently a fair number of men, discounting the Humbert Humberts, *can* appreciate a woman athlete's appeal, even if they're not too interested in the quality of her performance. A woman named Katy Schilly remembers running a race at Madison Square Garden when she was on the University of Iowa track team. "Someone in the audience started wolf-whistling at me," she says. "I was in fifth place and should have been doing better, but for a moment I stopped pushing and thought, I don't have to win. I'm a girl and I'm pretty and that's what counts. Can you believe it? Here I was in the middle of a race, and I was glowing because some man I didn't know thought I was sexy. I thought, Katy, you'd better snap out of this." One film casting director sympathizes with the man in the audience. "Women athletes have a kind of unbridled sexuality," he says. "This is going to sound sexist, and I'm sorry, but a man watches an athlete throwing her body around and all he's thinking is that she'd be a whole lot of fun in bed."

Sex Objects, Idols, and Scandals

It was probably inevitable that a sex scandal would erupt sooner or later in women's sports, and when it did, Chuck Debus was a likely person to be involved. A good-looking bachelor in his mid-thirties, Debus was at the center of a controversy at the University of California, Los Angeles, in which ill feeling and million-dollar lawsuits almost blew apart one of the best women's sports programs in the country. Debus was already coach of the women's track and field team at the school when Judith Holland was hired as the women's athletic director in July 1975. As a condition for accepting the job, Holland, a tough-minded administrator, had demanded the right to choose her own coaching staff. She reviewed Debus's record and decided to rehire him. "He had led the team to two national championships," she recalls, "and while I'd heard a few nasty rumors, there was nothing sufficient to make me say 'I don't want him.'" But a few months later, that's exactly what she did say. Debus's admirers insist that Holland just wanted to get rid of the coach and relied on sexual innuendo to discredit him. The anti-Debus forces claim that the coach was a hothead and liar who took advantage of women athletes' sexual insecurities and deserved to be fired.

The first charge against Debus involved Julie Brown, a lovely runner with Olympic hopes who had credited Debus with cutting fifty seconds off her mile time. Julie had spent the summer traveling with the U.S. National Track Team and was at an important Russian-American meet in Durham, North Carolina, when she was thrown off the team and sent home—charged with spending the night in a motel room with Chuck Debus. "This was all fully admitted," says Holland. "The explanation given was that the dorm situation was bad and Julie wanted to get away. Well, I don't care what went on in that motel room, but when it becomes widely known that one of my coaches got a girl kicked off a national team, I have to say something's wrong." That it should be anybody's business where athletes spend their nights is in itself a scandal, but at Durham, the women were expected to stay together in a dormitory and work out only with the team coach, not their own. "Julie was used to training with Chuck, so of course she wanted him nearby at the Russian meet," says one runner. "Judie Holland should be grateful that he had enough dedication to go there, take her running, and ignore the stupid rules." Further intimations of impropriety arose when Pat Connolly, an older track star and longtime acquaintance of Debus, heard a few women on the team claim that he had made sexual advances to them. She brought the women to see Holland, and they repeated the charges. That did it; Holland called Debus into her office and demanded that he resign.[2]

In the months that followed, Debus sued to get his job back, and there was much speculation about the power plays that had led to his ouster. Some suggested that Pat Connolly, the woman who took over the coaching job, had conspired against him.[3]

2. Holland wanted winning teams, but she also wanted to clean up the sullied reputation of UCLA sports. She had vowed to run her program "ethically and morally," and felt personally affronted to hear that Debus was scoring with his athletes off the field as well as on. Also, Holland was upset when UCLA lost a bid to host the 1977 women's track championships because the AIAW didn't want Debus as meet director. Shortly after he resigned, the AIAW reconsidered and gave the meet to UCLA.

3. Pat Connolly had been coach for women's track and field in the early seventies when the school had no official team. She had trained briefly with

But the really amazing point was that when Debus left, nine-teen women quit the team, refusing to train with a different coach. During the next year, threatened with a loss of financial aid, some of them returned; but eventually five women relin-quished their athletic scholarships, and three of them—includ-ing Julie Brown—left the university to train elsewhere with Debus. Even if it's true that Debus was having sexual affairs with women on his team, it would be stretching credulity to suggest that he had been intimate with all nineteen of his loyal-ists. But Debus was able to resolve the women's conflicts about being jocks, making them feel that their desirability increased with their athletic prowess. "We shouldn't have been compet-ing just to get an attractive man's approval," says one woman, "but Chuck paid a lot more attention to you if you were doing well. You spend your whole life hearing that you must be a lesbian because you're a jock, and then a Chuck Debus comes along and understands that it doesn't work that way at all. Of course we didn't want to give him up." Pat Connolly echoes her sentiments. "He could make you feel like the neatest, sexiest broad ever. When he said, 'Hey, baby,' you listened."

Women who dabble in sports may find that their sexuality increases as they get to like their bodies, but some talented athletes, particularly in male-dominated sports like track and field, still worry that success will make them unacceptable to men. The UCLA nineteen latched on to Debus because he loved winners and fought for them. "I understand how they felt," says Pat Connolly. "I got married for the first time because I wanted a man to prove that I was all right. I was sick of hearing derogatory remarks about my muscles and I was terribly inse-cure about my sexuality." Connolly resents anyone who ex-ploits women's qualms. "I'm a red-blooded athlete and I like sex," she says. "I'm a very physical person. And if women would think about it, they would realize that all sports can do

Debus, whom she called a "close confidant," and recommended him for the coaching job when she left the area. She insists that she said to him, "Chuck, don't mess around with any of the girls, okay?"

is make them more hot-blooded than before. They don't need to become pawns."

After the Debus affair, some young women began looking at their male coaches with a more skeptical eye, wondering about their motives. Judith Holland warned that dependence on a male coach was common but dangerous. "The women are still feeling their way and they don't have any faith in themselves," she says. "They build up an almost religious devotion to a coach, which is a very bad idea." It's true that male athletes also get dependent on their coaches for advice and guidance, but the situation is different. "Men like coaching women because they can control them," says marathon runner Frank Shorter, an Olympic gold medalist. "The women don't have much sports background, and they're ripe to have someone come in and dominate them. That's great for a coach's ego. He can tell them to do anything and they never stop and say, 'What is this bullshit? I know what I should do.' "

Laura Craven, a remarkable runner who dreams about "someday catching Frank Shorter," decided to train without a coach at all. At age twelve, Laura was so tiny and frail-looking that most men would have been wary of letting her cross the street alone, never mind run several miles alone down country roads. But that year she ran her first marathon and finished near the front with her long braids flying and her skinny legs kicking high. The coaches at a track club in her hometown near Columbus, Ohio, wanted her to run sprints and short races. "They said I'd fall apart running long distances, but that's silly," she says. "You get to know yourself pretty well, and your body gives signs if you start to work too hard. It's also pretty obvious when you're loafing." Many a male coach, though, feels quite confident about telling a woman athlete that he understands the female body better than she does. Some of them spike their manipulation with callousness. Laura's mother once heard a respected coach explain that it was wise to run young girls as hard as possible and not worry about burning them out. "By the time they're fourteen they discover boys and quit track, anyhow," he said. Mrs. Craven was livid. "Male coaches don't believe that women have futures," she says. "All they want to do with girls on the junior circuit is win track meets."[4]

The old stereotype of woman jock as lesbian, which has led to so many problems, hasn't yet been eradicated. Whether homosexuality is more prevalent in the sports world than elsewhere is hard to say, though it's likely that the percentage of homosexual athletes is about the same as the percentage of gay lawyers, fire fighters, and physicians. Lately, several male athletes have confessed that, despite their supermacho image, they are homosexuals. These revelations have had surprisingly little impact. "We always leave the men alone and make a big deal about the women in sports who might be gay," says Dr. Thomas Tutko, a psychologist at San Jose State University. "A male athlete isn't going at a cross-cultural role, but the woman is. So everyone starts gossiping and wondering what sports has done to her private life." The slightest suggestion of a liaison between well-known women athletes has mothers pulling their daughters off the playing fields and into ballet class, sure that youthful rough and tumble would lead to sexual confusion or lesbianism. When Chris Evert decided to cut down on her tournament play in 1978, rumors circulated to sportswriters that (1) she was annoyed by the prevalence of lesbianism in tennis, or (2) she had just broken up with her (female) lover on the tour. Both stories were false, but they point to the kind of pressure and sneering which women athletes—even the most acceptable —often face. "A male athlete is glorified," says Dr. Tutko, "but think what happens to a girl. First she's called a tomboy, then a freako, then a lesbian. I have tremendous respect for the women pros who make it to the top, because they have a

4. A young woman doesn't get "burned out" just by running a lot, but problems arise when she is urged to train regardless of injuries. Permanently damaged knees and torn ligaments are common consequences. In one case, the star of a local girls' team in Ohio was out with a back injury, and the coach realized that his team didn't have much chance in the state meet if she remained on the sidelines. He asked the thirteen-year-old girl to run, not worrying that if she agreed and injured her back again, it would probably be the last time she ever ran. She chose not to run.

helluva lot more conflicts than most men can imagine."

Golfer Amy Alcott learned about those conflicts when she joined the professional circuit at age nineteen and immediately began winning money and losing friends. "Everyone assumes that golfers are dykes," she said then. "I do everything I can to look all-American and wholesome." A dark-haired, ordinary-looking young woman who was perpetually five pounds too heavy, Amy tried to promote herself as the new "girl next door" on the tour. "You have to get people to realize that you're normal; otherwise you're ignored, no matter how much money you win." Amy spent most of her rookie year alone in hotel rooms, talking long-distance to her family in California whenever she got forlorn. Loneliness is a common plight for women on a professional circuit. While most male athletes have "sports wives" who travel with them, married women athletes rarely have tag-along husbands. For single women, the independence can become trying. "You go into a new city, and you either try to get picked up at a bar or you spend your time in a hotel room," says one golfer. "After a while it's hard to say which is worse." A tennis player who dropped off the professional circuit after getting sick of existing out of a suitcase for months on end discovered that the male pros have their own solution to solitary travel. "The guys all have their groupies," she says. "They go to a tournament, wag a finger, and a pretty little girl comes to spend the night. New town, new bedmate. The women pros don't like playing that game." To avoid that, many of the women golfers and tennis players turn to each other for companionship, and that's when the rumors start. One year, stories of a war going on between the straight women and the lesbians on the golf circuit caused rampant bitterness; as a result, the directors of the Ladies Professional Golf Association hired an advertising man, Ray Volpe, as commissioner and asked him to change the women's image.

The LPGA was founded in 1949, nineteen years before the women's tennis circuit. But almost three decades later, the golfers were still receiving less money and more scorn than the

tennis players—possibly because the golf champs were generally older, and they had a reputation for being hard-bitten. That
wasn't helped when a female reporter for the *Washington Star*
claimed in an article that the percentage of lesbians in the LPGA
was well above the national average and that the number included many of the top pros. Carol Mann, the bright, 6′3″
president of the LPGA, suggested that many country clubs were
refusing to sponsor events because of the assumption that
members of the tour were lesbians. "These are upper-class,
white clubs," said one player, "and they don't want dykes on
the fairways." Mann asked all the women on the tour to adopt
a straight life-style "for the sake of everybody."

Ray Volpe immediately recognized that in golf, as in many
other sports, it was going to take a charmer rather than a champion to get the sport accepted. Volpe thought he'd found his
savior in Laura Baugh, a pretty, shapely young player who
hadn't won any of the major tournaments but did wear tight
T-shirts and colorful hats while she played. Stodgy male sports
reporters who were used to comfortable seats in baseball press
boxes would drag themselves over to a women's event only if
they thought something very special would happen. Looking at
blonde Laura was considered very special. The older women on
the circuit who had struggled for years without recognition
were occasionally annoyed that flashbulbs began popping only
when Laura was around, but they understood that it was just
one more indignity to be faced. "We're all benefiting from
Laura's good looks," said one chunky golfer resignedly. "If
newspapers only want to print pictures of perky blondes, well,
they've got their perky blonde. The publicity won't hurt."
Volpe agreed. And if he had been able to create one on his
sketch pad, Volpe couldn't have found a better follow-up to
Laura than Jan Stephenson, a blue-eyed, blonde Australian who
one sports reporter said brought "sex to the sand traps." Jan also
managed to place well in some big events. *Sport* magazine featured her on the cover of its May 1977 issue, the first time in
history that the magazine had a cover girl. The picture came as

close to being a pinup as that magazine dared and revealed a good deal of Jan's breasts. With a glint in his eye, Volpe later explained that the picture had "good sexual overtones." But Jan, unaccustomed to being a sex symbol, appeared in his office in tears, asking what she should do about such exploitation. He told her to enjoy it. "Madison Avenue uses sex to sell soap and soup and cars, so why not use it to sell golf?"

Volpe continued to promote the heterosexual ideal by dreaming up things like the $200,000 Mixed Team Championship. The first year of the coed play, each woman was told to invite one of the players from the men's tour to be her partner. Nearly all the top male pros agreed to participate in this cross between a golf match and a Sadie Hawkins Day dance, even though very few of them were acquainted with the women who lured them to tees. Certain prejudices did get cleared away. One good male player, Chi Chi Rodriguez, admitted that he expected his blind date to weigh about 200 pounds and hold her putter backward. But the voice on the phone turned out to belong to JoAnn Washam, a 110-pound powerhouse who won (with Chi Chi) the $40,000 first prize. And although the television networks had been assiduously avoiding women's golf, the boy-meets-girl format was intriguing enough to get the cameras rolling.

Some athletes have had to do more than get a date to prove their sexual normalcy. Women who competed internationally in the late 1960s remember the sex tests in which they were required to take off their clothes and let a panel of doctors stare at them for a while to determine whether or not they were real women. The women's joking while they stood in line for the sex checks belied the anguish that many of them felt. Before one track and field meet, a flat-chested woman runner stood nude in front of the doctors for what seemed like an unusually long time. One of them kept muttering something she couldn't understand and finally the woman sputtered, "Doc, if I flunk this test, you're going to have to explain it to my three kids." Sex tests at the Olympics and other international competitions are now standard, but less embarrassing: A lab technician scrapes the inside of the cheek and peers at the collected cells under a microscope to check the chromosome count. The procedure itself is painless, but the psychological implications often hurt. "It's a way of saying: 'If you're this good in sports you can't be a real woman,'" says Thomas Tutko. Being forced to prove one's sex can be unnerving. Some shot-putters and javelin throwers admit that they've gotten nervous before the test, secretly wondering if their puissance is indeed the result of some biological quirk. "What's ridiculous is that you have to keep taking the test at every meet," says one athlete. "Isn't once enough?" When Debbie Meyer was preparing for the Olympics at age sixteen, the idea of taking a sex test got her more panicked than any of her competitions. "I hadn't had my period yet," she says, "and I started worrying that maybe there was something wrong with me. She had her private doctor in California perform a chromosome evaluation before the Olympics, to reassure her that she hadn't trained herself out of being female.

Not all athletes have Debbie's foresight. The 1972 Olympics was a morass of mix-ups for American athletes: Some male sprinters were disqualified because their coach had the wrong starting time for their heat; a male swimmer was stripped of his medal, accused of "doping" because his allergy medicine turned up in a urinalysis; and diver Janet Ely had a sex problem. Because of a misunderstanding, she was never told to take the chromosome test, and just a half hour before she was to dive, she was threatened with disqualification. She rushed to the ominously named Sex Control Station. German doctors began babbling over their microscopes, and sixteen-year-old Janet, instead of thinking about back somersaults and swan dives, began to worry about her sex. "I thought, Oh my God, maybe I am a boy," she reported later. The problem her jittery mind kept replaying was that she had a twin brother. Could it be that somehow, who knows how, they were identical instead of fraternal twins? Had her brother's egg contaminated hers? The scene belonged to the Theater of the Absurd—a talented woman diver at her first Olympics forced to stand around thinking about what egg she'd come from. Janet was eventually exonerated and allowed to go back to the swimming hall, reassured of being her brother's sister.

The only woman ever known to have failed a sex test was Ewa Klobukowska, a Polish sprinter and world record holder who was banned from a competition in 1967 on the ground that she had one chromosome too many. Her name was scratched from the record books, and her Olympic medals were invalidated. Some doctors complained that the ruling was unfair. It sometimes happens that an individual is born with male and female sexual characteristics, and doctors try to determine immediately their "true" sex. In Ewa's case, the male gonads had been removed and she was given female hormones and raised as a female. "In such cases it's possible for the genetic and anatomical sex not to agree," says Dr. Clayton Thomas. What gives a male an advantage in strength is male hormones, not chromosomes. But because hormone levels are radically different in various individuals, it's nearly impossible to draw the line on what hormone content is "female" and what "male." Since male and female hormone counts both form bell curves over each sexual population, the hormonal makeup of some men and some women overlap. Despite her extra chromosome, Ewa probably functioned more as a female than other genetically correct women who take steroids (male hormones) for strength.

The idea for a sex check possibly arose in 1955, when a German who had won a world record in the women's high jump seventeen years earlier admitted that he was a man and claimed he was forced to pose as a woman by the Hitler Youth Movement to win medals for the glory of Germany. In 1966, the sex review was initiated at the European track and field championships in Bucharest, and the more than two hundred women who pulled off their clothes for the judges were all certified as females. But six world-class athletes, including four Soviets, didn't appear. Missing from the test area—and from the games —were Soviet shot-putter Tamara Press and her sister Irina, a

hurdler. Newspaper stories had earlier speculated that the mas-
culine-looking Press sisters were really the Press brothers; even
now nobody is really sure.

More controversy about what makes a woman a woman
stirred when Renee Richards, a transsexual, began to play
women's professional tennis. Renee had once been Richard
Raskind, a male ophthalmologist and tennis player, and the
reaction against her was tumultuous. At the first major tournament that she entered, the Tennis Week Open in New Jersey,
most of the top pros withdrew in protest. A *Sports Illustrated*
reporter lamented in print that she had no right to be there: "A
6'2" former football end in frilly panties and gold hoop earrings
pounding serves past defenseless girls? . . . Who ever heard of
such a thing?" With all the champions gone, one of those defenseless girls, a seventeen-year-old junior player, beat Renee
easily in the semifinals. The defeat didn't discourage Renee, nor
did it ease the vociferous complaints from opponents, who
continued to stomp off the court at other tournaments rather
than play her. By blurring the lines between male and female
athletes, Renee Richards was unintentionally intimating what
many had secretly feared, anyway—that women in professional
sports are slightly tainted and, gold hoop earrings or not, full
of masculine impulses. "Actually it's the opposite," says one
tennis player. "We're proud to be women and don't want anyone questioning our sex."

In other sports, women have learned that the best way to
survive is to flaunt their sexuality. At one all-girl rodeo, the
sponsor held a cowgirls' beauty pageant and promised checks
of $250 to the winner and $50 to the runners-up. "We've got
to prove to everyone that cowgirls don't always look like their
horses," explained the rodeo director. He figured that getting
some skin pictures into the local newspaper would attract more
fans to the rodeo. The cowgirls were wary, but he was blunt—
they had to do this or there'd be no prize money. That evening
eight cowgirls put on bathing suits (one left on her boots, another her hat), swallowed a few shots of scotch, and were

cajoled to the outdoor stage. Choosing the winner was easy; the head judge, a famous old-time cowboy, said resolutely, "I only like cowgirls with nice boobs."

Rodeo is more than a sport; it's a part of Western culture, and for years, cowboys have loaded wives, kids, horses, and dogs into their trailers and followed the rodeo circuit as it wends up and down the California coast and into Wyoming, Oklahoma, and Utah. After a while some of the wives decided they wanted to do something at the rodeos other than stay in their trailers; so by smiling a lot—or doing whatever else was necessary—they got one event, barrel racing, accepted into a scattering of rodeos.[5] Eventually the more tenacious members of the Girls Rodeo Association began thinking that they could survive without being indulged by condescending cowboys, and they inaugurated all-girl rodeo.

There are seven events in all-girl rodeo, including calf roping, bull riding, and bareback bronc riding. Roping takes the most skill; riding the wild livestock demands the most guts. If there were more all-girl rodeos with decent pay, there'd be more good cowgirls—but when many of the women taste their independence, they get scared. "Without the men supporting us we'd starve to death," says Kay Vamvaros, a small cowgirl who wears big hoop earrings. One longtime GRA executive agrees. "The only way we got into the rodeos at all was by looking good," she says. "I keep reminding the girls that we'll be in only as long as we don't make too much trouble and give the men what they want."

All-girl rodeos might have drifted forever in nonpaying obscurity if a public relations executive from Los Angeles named Laurance Laurie hadn't heard about them and become convinced that the spectacle of 95-pound girls riding ton-weight bulls would attract publicity. One of his clients, a land developer in the West, agreed to put up a few thousand dollars in

5. In barrel racing, horse and rider dash around three empty barrels set in a cloverleaf pattern. A well-trained barrel horse is very expensive and hard to find, and is as important for success as a good rider.

prize money—enough to attract the best cowgirls in the country —and proclaim the event the world championship. The young cowgirls loved it; they got money, rough-riding, and attention. Laurie's client loved it, since the reporters who flew in from around the country mentioned his development in their stories. But the bliss wasn't pervasive. Traditionalists in the GRA shuddered at this breaking away from the cowboys. Even now, the organization's directors, many of them married to cowboys of the old breed, remain convinced that the women's job is to be ornamental at men's rodeos. They devote much of their energy to writing dress codes and issuing fines to cowgirls who ignore them. When one rebel faction objected to wearing expensive pants into the muddy rodeo rings, the directors were unsympathetic, explaining that cowboys wear blue jeans, but cowgirls don't. "We used to make the girls wear lamé outfits, but we've toned it down a little," says Kay, who was president of the GRA. "As long as the outfits are colorful and coordinated, we don't say much."

With its emphasis on clothes and style, the GRA newsletter tends to function as a mud-splattered *Women's Wear Daily*. One issue warned: "Girls . . . WE HAVE REALLY BEEN SLIPPING A LITTLE IN OUR APPEARANCE." The writer outlined offenses: "A few bad habits . . .

1. Sheer see-through blouses
2. No bras on some girls who need them
3. Drab colors that don't match and faded denims
4. Baggy pants
5. Tacky-looking hats"

Kay recommended that the newsletter print a "Bad Dressers of the Month" list. The unwritten message in the newsletter was that if the cowgirls wore more makeup and prettier clothes and lavished a bit more charm on the cowboys, they'd be better paid for barrel racing and could forget about their all-girl rodeo nonsense. "The young girls think they can be independent," says a married cowgirl named Butch, "but what they don't understand is that the judges couldn't care less about how they ride. They give a girl extra points for looking nice or being a good lay."

Some of the cowgirls remain undaunted. "The younger ones are fearless," says a high-spirited, bronc-riding mother of seven named Jan Edmundson. "They're not scared of the bulls, and they're not scared of what men'll say about them. I'm so old that I'm not scared of those things, either." More typical of the emboldened cowgirls are the Pollard sisters, three teenagers from Bassett, Nebraska, who invaded the macho world of bull riding without a tremor. At one championship Annette Pollard, the best rider and the prettiest of the three with her long blonde hair, skinny body, and delicate features, looked scornfully at the large crowd in the stands and told me not to be impressed. "A lot of men come to rodeos hoping to see a pretty girl fall on her head," she said. An hour later, her older sister Ralena did just that and ended the day with a double skull fracture. "I don't know about Ralena," said Annette with a shake of her head. "She must have a weak skull." The new cowgirls aren't used to being coddled.

Even for the intrepid, handling the cowboys can be frightening. The rule of the road is that a cowboy can sleep wherever he likes, but when he stumbles home at 6:00 A.M., his wife is supposed to be there. "You know before you get married that all cowboys chippy," says one wife who sometimes enters the barrel races. "My husband has had I don't know how many dozen women since we've been married. I don't sleep around because I don't want to and I don't dare. I suppose I should throw him out on his butt, but he makes good money and he makes good love. What would I do if he left?" On the road, traveling hundreds of miles to rodeos, the younger cowgirls get wise quickly. "I meet these cowboys and they all want to screw me, so they give me a ring and say we're going steady," says Annette. "Well, I know what those rings mean to them, so they mean the same to me. Every night I put them in a box and go out dancing."

Cowgirls aren't the only athletes who still get the discrimination blues. Maybe it has something to do with the interplay of men and horses and women, but in terms of dollars won and dignity lost, the racetrack is nearly as fiendish as the rodeo circuit. Women who want to be jockeys get caught in a sexual power play where cash and egos are on the line. One young jockey named Donna Hillman quit racing after a few years around the tracks, insisting that the only way a woman jockey could succeed was by playing sex games with the owners. "I'm not willing to do that, so I might as well forget about riding," she said. Some of the other women jockeys retorted that the charge was bunk. "Maybe she couldn't make it on her own merits," snapped one, "but some of us can."

For a while, women jockeys were a novelty and, as one male track fan claims, they were like dirty movies: Everybody had to see just one. They got a lot of publicity, and the best ones—like Robyn Smith and Mary Bacon—got offers to do television commercials and pose nude in *Playboy*. Eventually that got them more publicity but not more mounts. Reporters exploited the *National Velvet* angle of the pretty girl in riding clothes with dirt smudged on her cheeks finding happiness with a horse. It worked for Elizabeth Taylor, but in real life it was too good to be true—and most of it wasn't. After a while the women stopped adhering to their packaged image and complained about discrimination, loneliness, and pain. Mary Bacon announced her allegiance to the Ku Klux Klan. Robyn Smith admitted that everything she had said about her former career as a Hollywood starlet was a lie.

Robyn was one of the first women in the country to get a jockey's license, in 1969, and within a very short time, even the most hardened critics admitted that she could make a horse respond. But she didn't often get the chance, since the owners, nearly all men, didn't trust a woman on their expensive animals. During her first seasons in New York racing, Robyn had exactly sixty-seven mounts, while male jockeys of comparable skill and experience generally went to the gate more than a thousand times. Her first mount was Exotic Bird, a horse famous for finishing last in every race he entered; under Robyn's whip he was barely nosed out of the money. "A good horse runs at about forty miles per hour," says Robyn, "but honestly I think some of mine couldn't go faster than twenty-five."

Despite her high winning percentage, no agent would represent her ("A woman's got to sell herself," explained one) and so Robyn appeared at the racetrack every morning at dawn to exercise horses and appeal to trainers to let her ride. Then came her big break. The rich uncle in this romantic tale turned out to be Alfred Vanderbilt, who insisted that she was "just plain good" and made her the regular rider for his horses. Most top jockeys and reputable stables have arrangements like this, but since a woman was involved, the rumors began to buzz around the barns like flies. Here was Alfred Gwynne Vanderbilt, millionaire, fiftyish, former chairman of the New York Racing Association, powerful and prominent, giving a chance to Robyn Smith, late twenties, background unknown. Robyn responded haughtily to the innuendos about their relationship, claiming that she was on good terms with Mr. Vanderbilt and even better terms with Mrs. Vanderbilt.

Nobody suggested that Robyn didn't deserve to ride the Vanderbilt horses, but that had nothing to do with the rumors. Constantly being hounded for interviews but unwilling to talk about her past, Robyn cheerfully gave everyone something different to write. The basic outline was that she had been an English major at Stanford, class of '66. Afterward, she was signed to a movie contract at MGM, where she became a party-going, fun-loving Hollywood girl. One day, tired of moviedom's exploitation and chicanery, she packed her bags and decided to try her luck as a jockey. It was a fine tale, but there were no birth or school records to corroborate it, nobody at Stanford had ever heard of her, and MGM officials said she might have once taken an open workshop class, but that was it. Robyn handled the new wave of reporters by closing the door of her virtually private quarters, the lady jockeys' room at Belmont Raceway. "Why can't people judge me for what I'm doing now?" she said to me once. "My personal business is mine, and believe me, it's not as interesting as my life as a jockey."

Whatever else is or isn't true about her background, Robyn didn't grow up with a "horsey" set and she didn't even get on her first horse until she was about twenty. From then on, whether she was escaping from a dismal past or running toward a dreamed-about future doesn't really matter: She had pertinacity and relied almost exclusively on her own grit and determination. Still, around the racetrack she is The Bitch. (As in "The Bitch is riding in the seventh. Sure bet.") Nobody has anything particular against Robyn; it's just that a woman at the racetrack is hard to understand but easy to stereotype. If, as the rumors claimed, Robyn has been trying to succeed on sexual wiles, she has a funny way of doing it. She appears at the track every morning in drab jeans, baggy sweaters, and no makeup. With her weight down to 102 pounds (she's 5'7") she looks gaunt rather than lithe. "Most jockeys weigh more than I do," she explains, "but sometimes a horse is given a special low weight advantage, and if you can make the weight, you can get the mount." Willing to sacrifice anything for a chance to be in a race, she lives on diet pills and yogurt and gets annoyed when anyone hints that she might look better with a few more pounds and a few more curves. Most nights she's in bed by 9:00 P.M. and she never appears at the chic New York parties where wealthy owners pass their evenings. "An owner doesn't need any more socialites; he needs someone to win with his horses," she says.

With Robyn as a role model, hundreds of young girls now work at racetracks as stablehands and exercise girls. The pay is low, and many work for nothing to get experience. They're at the stalls at dawn to clean saddles and walk horses and rake manure, hoping that some trainer will notice their dedication and help them along. But "girls succeed here according to their looks," says one stablehand. "It's pretty, prettier, and prettiest, and you know who makes it. If you want to stop mucking stalls, you better be fucking the trainer." For years, girls weren't officially allowed near the barns at racetracks, but young girls with a passion for horses would sneak into the stalls at night and sleep in the hay near their favorites. "They'd do anything to be near the animals," says one old groom. "We'd find them here every morning and they'd jump up and run away." The decision to hire girls to do actual work in the barns came when two unions tried to organize the male stablehands and the trainers decided that hiring girls was better than increasing wages. Suddenly, there was competition for even the lowliest jobs. But union moguls may get another chance soon, since disillusionment is rampant in the backstretch at the racetrack. The trainers have been ruthless with their new power, and salaries are minimal, the work is hard, and the girls complain that the men try to take advantage of them.

A young woman named Patty Winn quit college in Kentucky to try her luck at Belmont ("They've got the best horses," she says), then left the track a year later to take a job as a secretary. "You see all these other girls at the track, and you figure, Why should anyone give *me* a chance? When you figure out why, you don't like it. Or at least I didn't." The attraction between girls and horses has often been chronicled but never fully understood. Most of the girls who work at the tracks want to be jockeys, and Patty, though bitter about her experience, thinks she understands it. "Some psychologists say that a horse is a girls' first sex object, but that's not right," she says. "It's just that a horse is something you can control, and it's about the only thing you can trust. And unlike the men around here, it loves you for yourself."

Slowly, men are realizing that loving a woman athlete for herself isn't hard at all. "A woman who's happy with herself, making money, and not dependent on you for everything she does is naturally a good person to be with," says the husband of a pro golfer. The longtime male companion of a weight lifter agrees. "I suppose the men who are threatened by strong women stay away or demean them or make wisecracks," he says. "But let me tell you, they're really missing something special."

Chapter Five

Everyone Can Do It

If a thing is worth doing, it is worth doing badly.
—G. K. Chesterton

Interviewing women across the country about sports, I quickly realized that all those who aren't already on an exercise regime are planning to begin one soon. The problem is that the planners outnumber the doers. "Most women know by now that exercise is worthwhile," says a woman named Sally who leads classes at a well-known health spa. "You just have to give them the motivation to do it." Much of the motivation is suspect. Some health clubs exploit the idea of exercise-for-beauty without offering programs that can really make a woman feel alive. At one studio, the instructors wear black tights, high-heeled shoes, and very short skirts to lead the calisthenics classes. Most of the instructors are out-of-work actresses and models, and the exercises they teach are lackadaisical enough so that the two-inch heels scarcely matter. "If someone really wants to get something out of a class, I suppose she can," says Sally, "but generally it's a silly, social hour and our only goal is to make as much money as possible. The high heels are required, because they make it look like we have tight asses."

But many women now are avoiding such programs and discovering the real benefits of sports by experimenting with a variety of activities. "It's always been hard for me to develop a sense of self-sufficiency," says a twenty-eight-year-old computer sales representative from Cincinnati. "When I was younger, I had brothers and sisters to lean on, then my college sorority sisters, and now my husband. But when I'm out thwacking a tennis ball, I know it's all me." A woman in her mid-thirties who races motorboats off the coast of California also delights in what sports have done for her. "You start seeing yourself as a multidimensional personality," she says. "You develop a keener awareness of yourself and sharpen all your senses." People who don't know her well can't imagine even-tempered Michelle splashing through the waves of the Pacific Ocean at sixty miles an hour. But she does it with an exuberance that makes it hard to believe that until two years ago she rarely ventured near the water. "I was probably the only woman in Southern California who never had a tan," she says. "But I'd never thought of myself as an athletic person, and when everyone else dashed off to the beach, I stayed home and read."

Unathletic women thinking about sports should keep two main facts in mind: (1) there's no sport a woman can't—or shouldn't—try, and (2) it's never too late to start. The transformation from klutz to world-class competitor isn't likely to take place much after age thirty, but most women (and men) are less interested in world records than in personal goals. Joan Ullyot, the physiologist, began jogging with her husband to combat an over-thirty sagging stomach. After a while, she would keep running after he had gone home to have a few beers, and she's now a world-class marathoner. Most women under forty-five who are basically healthy can train themselves to run a nonstop mile within about two to three weeks. Begin with a walk-run exercise of twenty minutes, five times a week. Run as much as possible, even if it's only a hundred yards to start, and walk when breathing is difficult. The main point is to keep moving vigorously for the entire time. "I set out to prove that all the running books were crazy and someone as out of shape as I was would never be able to run a mile," says a Vermont schoolteacher. "Okay, I was wrong. Running a mile may not be a big deal, but for me, it means I've done the impossible." In Hawaii, the Department of Parks and Recreation holds a marathon clinic every Sunday for the nine months preceding the Honolulu marathon. Dr. Jack Scaff, who runs the clinic, insists that anyone who follows his plan will complete the marathon. More than six hundred women annually enter the event, and about 95 percent make it to the finish line.

Other sports provide a similar emotional boost. A Cambridge, Massachusetts, dental technician swims a mile a day at one of the nearby colleges or a local YMCA. She began swimming again at age twenty-nine, after a fifteen-year hiatus when she was ordered to stay out of the water because of middle ear infections. She finally had a skin graft operation on her eardrum and was told that if she took precautions, she could go into the water again. "I wear lambswool in my ears and a bathing cap, and I'm not allowed to submerge my head completely because the pressure can be dangerous," she says. "But it's worth it because the swimming is such a release for me. I've had a lot of medical problems which required hospitalization, like a tumor on the ovary. Swimming isn't going to help any of them, but at least I *feel* like I'm doing something positive to keep myself healthy. So many things aren't in your control that when you can do something that makes a difference in how you feel, you should."

No matter what sport they pursue, many women say that the activity gives them a sense of power and of being in control of their own body and destiny. A history professor who spent a year in England teaching and recovering from a divorce was cajoled into joining a faculty crew team. "For a while I thought those six A.M. workouts would kill me," she says, "but I really got to love them—especially when I realized that I wasn't brooding as much. Now I'm convinced that much of my angst was the result of flabby muscle tone." Being part of an eight-oared shell, rowing in perfectly synchronous motion down a sun-drenched river, is a thrill in itself. And it's hard to feel sorry for yourself when you're glowing from exertion and every muscle is throbbing.

Finding the time to exercise isn't really that difficult. "Just when you're the busiest is when you need sports the most," says Dr. Tenley Albright, the former skating champion. "A fit person needs less sleep. Her endurance, reflexes, and ability to think are better. When you're under stress or very pressured you need those traits, so taking time out to do something like skating or tennis isn't silly, it's vital." Tenley juggles her many commitments so that she can skate several times a week. "Sometimes it alarms me how free I feel on the ice," she says. "I forget the hospital and the groceries and the kids, and I'm just moving to the music. Everyone needs an emotional release like that." One young mother who, like Tenley, often goes to the Boston Skating Club, says that she used to feel guilty about taking time to skate instead of rushing home after work to be with her children. "But it was actually my kids who decided I should skate," she says, laughing. "When I'm not active I get tense and snappy. An hour on the ice and I'm a different person. I think my six-year-old sensed that I didn't yell at her as much when I'd been skating. One day she said, 'Mommy, if I get to play every day, how come you don't?' We think we're making these great sacrifices for our children, when what we're actually doing is sacrificing our children and ourselves for some principle which isn't correct to start with. Women shouldn't forget how to play."

The mental benefits of exercise are just beginning to be understood. A woman who once worked in the beauty department of a national magazine remembers the endless articles she wrote urging women to take time for themselves. That usually meant a few hours for a pedicure, sauna, or facial—all guaranteed to revive the spirits. Those time-out tricks may get a woman away from her screaming kids for a while, but they really don't do much to change her mind-set. That's not so for sports. Doctors now suspect that sports activities are more than "time away."

Reasonable training can affect mood and emotions and even stimulate the mind to new patterns of awareness. People involved in intense activity often report creative breakthroughs or flashes of insight that they can't explain later. "Whenever I have writer's block I go out running," says a novelist. "I think I get half my ideas on the go." This phenomenon actually has a scientific explanation. The left hemisphere of the brain is believed to be the rational, productive part of the mind, while the right hemisphere controls the intuitive, psychic, and creative flow. Surrendering to the natural rhythms of the body during exercise allows the mind to tune out the thinker and let the right hemisphere—and a whole new consciousness—take over.

Michael Murphy, the founder of Esalen and now chairman of the board, says that exercise is a kind of Western yoga. "The mind experiences that athletes report are similar to those of yogis during meditation," he says. Murphy studied in the 1950s at an ashram in India where he practiced meditation for eight hours a day. He founded Esalen at Big Sur in the fall of 1962, and eleven years later he introduced the Esalen Sports Center and began running daily himself. "Talk about the human potential movement has always concentrated on spiritual enlightenment," he says, "and it's time to bring the body back into it. There's so much about body-mind integration that we don't understand. I think it's our next great frontier and just as exciting as the space program." Dozens of athletes have cooperated with Murphy in exploring the changed state of awareness that sports can promote. "With a sympathetic listener, a few beers, and a very rare moment, people will tell me amazing stories about body experiences that they can't explain," he says. "Afterwards, they're embarrassed that they've mentioned it. We generally suppress the sublime and uncanny, and we don't even have the words to express some of the mind states that intense activity can induce." Carrie Graves, who rowed on the U.S. Olympic crew team in 1976, recalls moments of epiphany during particularly hard workouts. "I was pushing myself a hundred and ten percent," she says, "and all of a sudden the pain was gone and I felt very peaceful. It seemed that I knew things about myself most people never realize. It wasn't intellectual discovery, but it was suddenly understanding myself as a being." Another rower describes a feeling of harmony and flow at certain moments. "You're not thinking about what you're doing, but you're aware of being in sync with yourself and the environment. There's incredible power in that. You're almost omnipotent."

While Murphy is exploring the transcendent states that can be realized through body-mind flow, some psychiatrists have been studying the more apparent effects of exercise on the mind. In San Diego, Dr. Thaddeus Kostrubala often takes his patients running during sessions because he finds that they're able to let down barriers and talk more freely while running than when sitting in an office. He suggests that during exercise, thought patterns and hidden memories are freed. Exercise therapy has been particularly successful in treating cases of depression. "When you're depressed you keep turning inward," says one woman who has worked with Dr. Kostrubala, "but exercise gets you out of yourself, and you stop the endless ruminating."

Dr. Robert Brown, a Virginia psychiatrist, believes that much of the change is purely physiological. Depressions are often caused by an imbalance in the chemical substances that serve as transmitters between neurons in the brain. Most antidepressant drugs work by changing the concentration of chemicals in the body. Exercise may produce the same results as these drugs, without the side effects. "Nature has provided us with a natural way of keeping our body chemicals in balance," says Dr. Brown. The World Health Organization reports that roughly 10 percent of the population suffers from depression, making it the most prevalent disease in the world. About 70 percent of the patients who consult psychiatrists are depressed, as are one-third of all college-age women. Brown has found that exercise can relieve many depressions. When he administered objective tests to members of a women's tennis team before the season began, 40 percent of the players showed signs of clinical depression. After the season, the number had dropped to 23 percent. With the members of a women's softball team, 35 percent were depressed before they began the season's workouts and only 12 percent were depressed after. Equally significant was the fact that nearly all the women at the "nondepressed" end of the scale before the season moved even closer to zero depression once they had been exercising regularly.

Dr. Herbert DeVries, a physiologist at the University of Southern California, thinks that exercise can be more effective than tranquilizers in reducing anxiety. Working with the elderly, Dr. DeVries found that a dose of exercise reduces tension better than most drugs or other relaxation procedures.[1] "Just taking time out doesn't have nearly the same effect as exercising," he says. "Moderate-intensity exercise is the way to go." With such information, major companies like General Foods and Xerox have been opening massive fitness centers for their employees, believing that on-the-job exercise sessions pay off with better work. The federal government is also getting into the exercise act, and at the Department of Justice everyone, from the attorney general to summer interns, is encouraged to participate in sophisticated fitness programs in the converted basement of the J. Edgar Hoover Building. Workers are given three hours a week off from their jobs for the activities. "Sure it's expensive," says one department spokesman, "but the taxpayers aren't being cheated. It makes more sense to spend money on exercise equipment than life insurance benefits."

Nobody has ever cured depression or achieved transcendence by jogging around the block once a week, but it's not necessary to be a superathlete in order to experience mind changes. Mike Spino, a runner and coach who has worked with Michael Murphy at Esalen, thinks that too often exercise becomes just an-

---

1. In his study, a brisk fifteen-minute walk reduced tension an average of 20 percent. Note that Dr. DeVries was working with elderly patients, so a brisk walk raised their heart rate to 40 percent of capacity. For younger people, more vigorous exercise is probably necessary to achieve the same result.

other part of an overstructured life. "People plug into work from nine to five, and they come home and plug into running from five-thirty to six," he says. "That's not what sports should be about. There's no joy in that." The pattern is particularly common among women, who frequently approach exercise as another chore to be efficiently dispatched. They know that exercise is important, so they take a daily dose of it with the same zest reserved for swallowing a One-a-Day vitamin pill.

Attitude often determines how successful you'll be in achieving mental benefits. "You should hook into the emotional level of what you're doing," says psychologist Ken Dychtwald of Berkeley, California, who has done extensive studies on body-mind correlations. "Realize that there are as many emotional as physical barriers restraining you, and you have to relax, let go, and think about them. You can't get a new body by putting your old self into it." A variety of therapies and pseudotherapies with names like Bioenergetic Analysis and Rolfing have arisen to teach people to confront hidden feelings and emotions through physical expression. The basic idea seems to be that if Freud was confused about what women want and need, it might have been because he had them lying on couches rather than moving about and expressing themselves. "You don't just think life, you feel it," says Ken Dychtwald. "If you want to play life differently, you have to change the instrument. You can't get the sounds of a violin out of a tuba."

If you're no good at sports, it may be that your mind is holding you back more than your body. Working at his Human Performance Laboratory, Dr. Laurence Morehouse has been studying what prevents people from doing more in sports. "We used to think that the limiting factors were things like power and force," he says. "But now we find that most people are operating with their brakes on because of tension and inhibitions." Tension causes the muscles to constrict and slow down, so when you worry about failing, you actually make it harder for yourself to succeed. You often perform best when you're not trying too hard. Paradoxically, the more at ease you are, the more power you might have because muscles aren't pulling in opposite directions. According to Dr. Morehouse, getting rid of muscular tension also makes most thinking and creative work more efficient.

Most women in professional or competitive amateur sports claim they participate because it's fun. Given the paucity of money and fame for all but a very few, the explanation seems valid. But women who dabble in sports during off hours often miss the sense of fun. They choose sports like running or swimming so that they can be alone and not embarrassed as they try to get in shape. To men, sports usually involve teamwork and camaraderie; they provide a means for playing out fantasies and being a superhero—even on a field with a dozen or so similarly mediocre players. But for some reason, team sports have always been less acceptable for women. Little girls play solitary sports like jump rope or jacks; teenagers get strong encouragement in gymnastics and swimming; and virtually the only career possibilities for women are in individual sports like tennis, golf, or skating. Several recent studies of executive women note that those with individual-sports backgrounds have never learned the rules of competition and risk-taking. In business, they have difficulty seeing themselves as part of a team effort and don't know how to function as one member of a group that's out to win. Accustomed to working alone, they take all failures personally. Girls from the fingers-in-the-dirt school who gambol on male turf early are later more suited than most women to continue playing with the boys as equals at board meetings and congressional hearings. Betty Lehan Harragan, a management consultant, says she urges businesswomen to stop practicing and start competing in whatever sport they choose. "Women have to learn about competition and developing a winning attitude," she says. "You don't destroy a game by competition—you add something to it, and you learn about life."

Any woman dipping her toes into sneakers for the first time deserves a support system. "You're afraid of getting hurt and being laughed at and looking like a klutz when you start," says one member of a women's rugby team in Los Angeles. "A woman always assumes that she's more inept than anyone else. Our team motto is 'Give it a whirl.' If you land on your ass we'll laugh, but we'll also help you up." This spirit of cooperation and female bonding is too often missing from women's sports, but when it does appear, the result can be invigorating. For example, a group of mothers in suburban Connecticut who were accustomed to driving their young sons to soccer practice every afternoon decided that since they were so good at forming carpools, they could probably be equally successful at forming their own soccer team. None of the women had ever played before, but the boys' coach offered a few tips, and pretty soon the women were running around in cleats and high socks, successfully kicking and blocking. "The kids thought we were crazy at first," says one of the mothers, "but now we're fairly respectable." In other communities, working women and at-home women join together for evenings of softball, soccer, or volleyball. "Most women have all sorts of negative thoughts when they start to exercise," says Mike Spino. "They figure they're too fat or they don't have the ability or they'll never improve anyway. Our culture makes it seem that if you're not number one in something, you should quit. But that's just foolish."

When a women's football league began in the Midwest, dozens of people—secretaries, executives, housewives, and professors—tried out for spots on the teams. Many of the women had never held a football before. The eventual star of the league was a 5'3" player for the Toledo Troopers named Linda Jefferson who attended practices between classes at Toledo University and a night-shift job at United Parcel Service. When *Women-Sports* magazine named her Athlete of the Year in 1975, she described herself as a "run-of-the-mill black girl." Her team was unbeaten for several seasons. For many of the Toledo women the problem of what to do with the kids was solved by taking them along. The children who ran around the edges of the field while their mothers practiced never seemed to bother anyone. Children were accepted all over the league. I watched once as a woman with long hair, shoulder and knee pads, and a helmet gently tossed a football to her very blonde five-year-old daughter. The little girl laughed excitedly, then watched with an intent gaze as her mother took the field. "When I grow up I'm going to be a football star, just like Mommy," she said.

For women who are still unnerved by such unconventional activities, aerobic dance centers are springing up across the country and dispensing cardiovascular conditioning along with Paul Simon tunes. The guru of the movement is Jacki Sorenson, whom the *Washington Star* described as a blonde who weighs "110 of the prettiest pounds you ever saw." An innovative dancer, Jacki once longed to dance professionally, and she never quite understood how exercise could be drudgery. "I think of my program as a whisper of exercise and a shout of fun," she says. Women at the aerobic dance centers all talk in exclamation points. The motto of the program is "Have fun! Keep fit!" and about 95 percent of the women who enroll for one twelve-week course return for another. Jacki devised the program in 1969 when she was living on an Air Force base in Puerto Rico with her husband, Neil. The bored-housewife syndrome is pandemic on military bases, and Jacki was asked to run an exercise program for wives. At the time, Kenneth Cooper's book *Aerobics*[2] was hitting the best-seller lists, and his program was used for fitness training by the Air Force. Aerobics improve general physiological condition by increasing the heart's ability to deliver oxygen. Any exercise which forces the body to use increased amounts of oxygen over long periods of time is aerobic. Dr. Cooper devised a point system, based on oxygen cost, rating different activities' efficacy in getting people into shape: For example, running a seven-minute mile is worth five points, cycling two miles in six minutes is worth three points. Thirty points a week are required for fitness.

2. Published in 1968 by M. Evans. *Aerobics II* (1968) was published as a Bantam paperback. Dr. Cooper has also written *The New Aerobics* (1970); *Aerobics for Women,* written with his wife, Mildred Cooper (1972); and *The Aerobics Way* (1977). All were published originally by M. Evans and later in paperback by Bantam.

In aerobic dancing, there's no talk about points or miles or minutes. The routines last until the music stops, and they combine dance movements like leg kicks and lunges with running, jumping, and jogging. "We don't worry much about skill and technique in teaching the dances," says one of the instructors. "The stated purpose is to have a good time." The studios have no practice bars or mirrors, so it's impossible to get self-conscious. Nobody wears tutus or ballet slippers, and the instructors, generally former students who decide they'd rather get paid than pay for the classes, never stop bouncing. They attend clinics every three months to learn the new dances that Jacki has choreographed. "I think of this as continuous entertainment, and everybody gets to be in the show," says Jacki. "Some of the women may not look like Ginger Rogers, but they feel like they do. They're just swinging wildly to the music and meanwhile getting into good shape." The classes all begin with one or two warm-up dances, continue with about twenty minutes of vigorous dance, and finish with cool-down exercises. Everything is done to music, including the sit-ups that are invariably scheduled into one of the warm-ups. "Nothing else is as good for the abdominal muscles," says Jacki, "but if you tell women to do thirty sit-ups, they groan. When they do it to music and clap their hands, they don't even realize how many they're doing."

Some of the dances have enough finger snapping, hand clapping, and hollering to make them downright hokey, but the larking is part of the appeal. Aerobic dance made its first commercial appearance in 1971 when Neil was transferred to New Jersey and Jacki decided to teach an aerobic dance class to six women in the basement of the South Orange YMCA. Within a year, the classes were a favorite morning pastime in South Orange, and the housewives didn't want to give them up when they heard that Jacki was being called to follow her husband again. So Jacki began flexing her still unused entrepreneurial muscles, formed the Aerobic Dance Corporation, and asked some of the women in the original class to work with her. "I didn't even know how to balance a checkbook before, and all

of a sudden I was part of a big business," says Connie Ridge-
way, a housewife who became vice-president of the corporation. "I had started the dancing classes after my third child was
born because I felt fat and flabby. But once you find out what
it feels like to be fit, you never want to stop." Jacki was proof
that solving the quivering thighs problem can change lives. Her
years of hopscotching around the world in the role of ever-loyal
wife ended when Neil quit his job to become chairman of the
burgeoning corporation.

Aerobic dance is no longer just a housewives' diversion. The
women who saunter into the aerobic dance studio on Park
Avenue in New York City at about 6:15 P.M. every day are
generally coming from their offices, and they're tired. Their
makeup is beginning to run and their energy is ebbing. They
don't talk much as they shove their designer clothes and Gucci
shoes into metal lockers and pull on shorts, T-shirts, and sneakers. "I need something to perk me up after work," says one
woman. "I used to head for a bar and have a couple of drinks.
Now I come here. Do you think that's crazy?" One businesswoman, Melanie Feder, attended classes five times a week at the
New York studio until she was invited to become an instructor.
"I've lost seventeen pounds and have twice as much energy as
I ever did," she says. "After twenty-nine years of doing nothing, I've been inspired."

Beginning any sport or exercise program requires a good deal
of faith in some unlikely truths: for example, that by expending
more energy you'll have more. An activity that puts demands
on the heart, lungs, and circulatory system makes your body
adept at using oxygen more efficiently. The more oxygen your
body can use, the more energy it can put out. When you work
harder than you ever have before, your body first gets exhausted from the overload, but eventually it becomes accustomed to functioning at a higher energy level. Your body works
only as effectively as it must to survive. "When people write
books claiming you can become fit with almost no effort, I ask:
'Fit for what?' " says Dr. Lenore Zohman, a cardiologist. "I

define fitness as a body economy that allows you to meet the physical and emotional demands of life with only modest effort." If your daily schedule involves a job sitting all day in an office, a few blocks of walking to and from a parking lot or bus stop, and mild activity at home in the evening, that's about all your system will be prepared to handle. An emergency that calls for long hours awake or extensive physical exertion will present almost impossible demands. However, if the same schedule is supplemented with an hour or so of brisk activity every day, the body is prepared for taxing conditions and primed to manage greater stress.

Women who haven't exercised much generally don't realize that the practice of conserving energy may work for fuel tanks but not for women's bodies. "I've never had much stamina," says a woman in her late forties, "so I used to take life pretty easy and reserve my strength for when I had something important to do. I figured I deserved a rest now that my kids were grown and gone." But getting ten hours of sleep a night and very little physical activity hardly prepared her for the hectic evenings when guests came or weeks when her children visited from college. "I'd get exhausted if I had to entertain or spend a long day shopping," she says, "so I got more and more cautious and figured I had to rest a lot or fall apart." A female doctor and friend finally convinced her that boredom and *lack* of activity were the more likely causes of her lassitude. Feeling tired at the end of a day doesn't mean that the body has been properly exercised. More often, it shows the opposite. A woman who has spent all day standing in front of a class or sitting at a desk might well feel tired by the evening and drop into bed at 9:30 P.M., feeling she merited her sleep. But if, instead, she took a brief rest, then headed to a discotheque (or at least turned on the radio) for some wild dancing, she'd actually be likely to feel more alive and energetic as a result. "After a hard workout, you're totally wiped out, but you feel great," says Linda Prefontaine, a professional racquetball player from San Diego. "It's like your body is clean and you've done something good for yourself." Adds another woman: "When I feel dragged out, it usually means I haven't been moving enough."

It takes only a day or two for the body to rebound from the most strenuous exercise, and longer rest periods are counterproductive, since conditioning benefits are lost very quickly. Experts estimate that after four weeks of not exercising, about 50 percent of cardiovascular conditioning is lost. When Dr. Barbara Drinkwater tested previously well-conditioned women after ten weeks without training, she found that their pulse rate, blood pressure, and aerobic capacity had reverted to pre-training levels. But while wind and endurance are lost easily, the muscles seem never to forget the skills that have been imprinted on them. A woman who knew how to ice-skate or ride a bicycle as a child will often be amazed twenty years later to discover that the techniques remain. One young woman who had played tennis regularly as a teenager picked up her racket again after a five-year hiatus. "For the first half hour I was thinking hard what to do, and I was awful," she reports, "but all of a sudden, everything fell together. It seemed that I didn't remember how to do a tennis stroke, but my muscles did."

The exhilaration of sports can come from all sorts of activities, and it's possible to get into excellent condition without doing dismal exercises. Women with diverse levels of skill are involved in mountaineering, rock climbing, ballooning, and kayaking. Women's expeditions have lately been tackling the major peaks in the Alps and the Himalayas—even Everest—and scared neophytes are beginning to venture where mother thought nice girls should never tred. "I led the most sheltered life you can imagine," says a young woman from Illinois named Polly Richards. "I was scared to death of everything and I wasn't athletic. The summer I went on Outward Bound really turned things around. I came home tanned, with muscles in my arms, and feeling good. I remember thinking, I did it! Me—Polly the klutz—I didn't give up!"

Outward Bound is one of several survival-training programs that are teaching women new things about themselves. Although they were once for men only, Outward Bound programs now offer wilderness experiences to thousands of people of both sexes over age sixteen, with many groups exclusively for adults and women. "It's interesting to lead coed groups," says one male instructor, "because the women unconsciously expect that we'll take care of them. But the wilderness is a great equalizer. Everyone is struggling, and once the women figure out that they've got to make it themselves, they do." The training may involve canoeing through Minnesota lakes, bicycling through the Blue Ridge Mountains, or sailing off the coast of Maine; but the real purpose of all of it is to build a sense of confidence and self-sufficiency.

Polly Richards recalls the first time her all-woman group went rock climbing and she was taught rappeling—being lowered down the side of a sheer cliff—while Lake Superior crashed against the rocks several hundred feet below. Hanging on by her fingernails and toes, with only a rope around her waist for security, Polly was terrified and began screaming and crying for help. "I was hysterical for about a half hour, and I had zero strength in my body from all the crying," she says. "But my instructor called down that tears wouldn't get me anywhere, and I finally pulled myself together and finished." The group spirit sustained Polly through her first miserable days, even though her initial reaction to the physical challenges was negative. "Most times in my life I'd say, 'I can't do that,' and then give up before giving myself a chance," she says. But when the other women—also jelly-kneed at first—tried something and succeeded, they exuberantly encouraged Polly. She climbed a sixty-five-foot rope ladder, paddled a canoe through white water, and finally survived a three-day "solo"—a standard Outward Bound test in which each person is left alone with only the clothes she's wearing, a sleeping bag, a whistle, and pencil and paper. "I had been so weak and vulnerable that our leader was genuinely worried about leaving me alone," she says, "but by then I knew I could do it. I was so inspired that I spent the whole time writing about how I'd reorder my life back home. I've begun to feel that I can do anything if I'll only try." A thirty-five-year-old teacher from Detroit who participated in one of the special programs for educators detailed a similar breakthrough. "I realized that my life had been run on excuses," she says. "I'd always told myself that I was too weak or uncoordinated or inexperienced to venture into something. The truth was that I was plain scared of anything unknown—and nobody had ever said to me, 'Take a risk: it's good for you.' "

Outward Bound students are urged to keep journals during the program, and although the early pages are usually filled with whining, the endings tend to sound like inspirational novels. During her solo, one teenager, Molly Lyren, described the small island she was on and admitted that she was scared. "But myself will keep me company," she wrote soothingly. "I guess that I'm not so afraid of other things as I am of myself. Maybe I'm afraid that I'll learn some things I won't like . . . but I can only feel better and less hesitant after this experience." A few months later, Molly admitted that she hadn't enjoyed Outward Bound while she was participating. Her arms ached from the exercise and she was constantly tired and often nervous. "But if you ask me now, I can only say I loved it," she insisted. "My confidence kept building, and even though my muscles got stronger, I think the biggest changes were mental, not physical. I feel comfortable about myself now. My parents notice the difference, and they're trusting me a lot more." Even the most pampered young girl is forced to learn responsibility in the wilderness. In coed groups, girls find that chivalry disappears under stress. One canoeist who insisted that she was too weak to portage the boat kept asking her male partner to do it. He was amiable for a while, but finally the extra load became too much. "Stop telling yourself all the things you can't do because you're a girl," he snapped. "Women don't lack strength; they're missing guts."

Sports that seem exotic or impossibly challenging probably aren't if you actually try them. One woman recalls her reluctance to join some friends on a hiking expedition, until someone described the activity as being nothing more than walking with some paraphernalia. In other words, anyone accustomed to lugging groceries home from the supermarket or carrying a baby around the house should be able to manage quite well hiking through Yosemite—with or without a backpack. Preferring flying over walking, women parachutists have performed difficult, free-flying tricks, and a novice can take her first jump after just a few hours of instruction. "I've always been terrified of airplanes," says a woman from Houston, "but on a vacation in Acapulco, my boyfriend convinced me to try sea-flying—you know, you're in the air with a kite on your back, but you're attached by a tow rope to a motorboat. It looks spectacular, but it's really easy and safe. Anyway, I got hooked on flying that way, and when we got back, I went to a parachuting school. I've taken two real jumps, and even if I never go back, I've proven something to myself forever. Some of my friends have decided I must be wonderfully brave. That's not true, but at least the 'fraidy cat is no more."

Denise Wiederkehr, a licensed balloonist from Minnesota, also has a reputation for daredevilry, since she has soared over mountains, lakes, and big cities. "But if you're careful about checking wind and weather conditions, there's not much danger in ballooning at all," she says. "My dad has flown over a thousand hours, and he's never even had a Band-Aid case." The best time for ballooning is dawn, while the winds are still calm and the sky is bursting with color. "You're in such harmony with the elements around the earth that you don't feel any turbulence," says Denise. "It's so peaceful that you forget all your problems." Floating blissfully along with the zephyrs and the birds, Denise once set a record by flying the 228 miles from Lakeland, Minnesota, to Waupon, Wisconsin, in 11 hours, 10 minutes. (It was a distance and time record.) The temperature that day was minus ten degrees, but she hardly noticed. "You're moving with the wind, so there's no chill factor. The sun was out, and I felt so warm and exhilarated that I even took off my gloves." Later, she was paid to pilot the Kentucky Fried Chicken balloon—a promotional balloon shaped like a chicken —which she flew over cities throughout the United States. "Ballooning is a gentle sport. When you're in the country, you can fly low and talk to the people on the ground. In the big cities at rush hour, everyone gets very excited when you pass overhead, and it's great advertising for a company. I mean, did you ever see anyone run after a billboard?"

Officials of the Balloon Federation of America say they didn't worry when women began rising in balloons. At one balloon festival I attended, several women were high in the sky, most as passengers in the gondolas. But as the sport becomes more popular, more and more women are getting licenses to handle the colorful balloons themselves. "I called myself a balloonist for years," says one woman pilot, "and all I had ever done was ride in the chase car. I finally realized—hey, I don't have to be grounded. Why should women always be the supporters? Now I'm the one who's high-flying, and I let other people follow me."

It takes hot air—and therefore a propane burner—to get a balloon flying, and skill rather than strength first to inflate and later to deflate and pack the balloon. I once watched a weekend balloonist land her colorful conveyance in a park, then tie it to a tow rope to give rides to the dozens of youngsters who rushed over, wide-eyed. It was mostly the small boys who pushed their way to the front of the crowd and held on to the rope, hoping to be chosen for the soaring venture. The girls hung back, several of them staring shyly at the slim pilot who knew exactly what to do with her dazzling toy.

"Can girls fly, too?" asked one eight-year-old finally.

"Girls can do anything," she said, popping the youngster into the basket for a ride.

Young kids can smell adventure and invariably want to be part of it, but girls who aren't encouraged to participate too often grow up and stop exploring. It doesn't have to be that way. Women who weren't given opportunities in sports when they were young are grabbing them now and developing prow- ess in diverse areas. For example, the first women's boxing bout was held in late 1975 in Virginia City, Nevada, and the winner was Caroline Svendsen, a thirty-four-year-old grandmother who had married at thirteen. "Sweet Caroline" knocked out her opponent in fifty seconds and was cheered by a thousand spectators who had paid five to seven dollars each to see the fight. Jim Deskin, the boxing commissioner in Nevada, had sanctioned the first women's fight grudgingly. "Might say women's lib got to me," he says. Despite court challenges and discrimination charges, liberation didn't get to many of the other commissioners, and more than three years later, women in several states were still battling, but not fighting. "The commissioners are afraid we'll degrade the sport," says Gwen Hibbler, a gentle-spoken pugilist, "but we're serious, and we're getting good."

Gwen grew up in Atlanta, Georgia, where she was one of about twenty blacks bused into an all-white school. "There were always fist fights after school," she says, "but I didn't want to hurt anybody and I didn't get involved. I just wanted to get my education and get out of there." Gwen eventually moved to New York, and when she didn't have enough money to stay in college, she got a job as a secretary at the Harlem Hospital. Eventually she met a woman boxer named Jackie Tonawanda (who used to be billed as "the female Muhammad Ali") and on a lark agreed to work out with her. Within a few years, Gwen was boxing professionally. "Before, I didn't think there was such a thing as a woman boxer," she says. "I figured I'd be a secretary forever. I guess it proves that you have to keep your eyes open and just go and take things from life." Elsewhere, other women are learning that the manly art of self-defense is a womanly art, too. In Texas, boxing programs for girls and women are proliferating, and some women's boxing clubs have also been started in Philadelphia. On the streets of Harlem, Gwen still prefers to run away from trouble rather than get involved in brawls, but even unused boxing skills offer some protection. "I never have any trouble any more," she says.

"Maybe men can see that they shouldn't start with me. You must walk different when you know you're not helpless."

Women in auto racing still hear jokes about lady drivers and find top manufacturers unwilling to sponsor them, but here, too, the route is being cleared. When Janet Guthrie competed at the Indianapolis 500 in 1977, famous male drivers like Bobby Unser told anyone who would listen that women are a menace on the track. Everyone else joined in speculating on how the president of Indy Speedway would modify the traditional opening, "Gentlemen, start your engines," for the first woman to compete.[3] Janet didn't particularly care. She felt more sorrow than pride in the "first woman to . . ." designation, since it pointed out how dreadfully hindered women had been previously. At her first Indy, Janet's green-and-white car kept sputtering, but through two hours of stifling heat, with a blistering fuel mixture that had spilled from the fuel tank seeping into her skin, Janet refused to quit. "I wouldn't have believed it," said one of her opponents, "but she's a real driver with real guts." When it was all over, *New York Times* columnist Dave Anderson watched her stride toward the showers, at last to wash away the painful alcohol and methanol mixture, and he just shook his head. "The lady belonged on the track," he wrote later. "She never even twitched." The next year, Janet competed with a broken wrist and finished eighth in the stellar field, outshining several previous winners and some of the top men in the sport. The publicity, criticism, and vitriol that had accompanied her earlier races began to disappear. "It's hard to say a woman can't drive when she's just blown your doors off," says Janet.

The men's alleged concern for the women's safety began to have a hollow ring when Shirley Muldowney started winning world championships in drag racing and Italian Lella Lombardi became competitive in Formula One, finished well in several

3. After much controversy, Tony Hulman, the seventy-six-year-old president of Indy Speedway, began the race by announcing: "In company with the first lady ever to qualify at Indianapolis, gentlemen, start your engines." A few months later, Hulman died, and the following year his widow, Mary, opened the proceedings with a simpler: "Ladies and gentlemen, start your engines,"

Grand Prix races, and along with a female partner, competed in the grueling twenty-four-hour race at Daytona. Now amateur women are racing stock cars and getting their licenses to compete in the big time. Doing that gets easier every year.

Women, even racers' wives, weren't allowed into the pits at Indy until 1973, so gaining experience around cars has been difficult. When Janet Guthrie competed in a race at Darlington Speedway, the identification tag she wore as a driver said "No Women Allowed." "Racing is a calling, a passion," says Janet. "I can't recommend it to women or anybody because you have to love it deeply before it's worthwhile. But if you do love it, you should try. You advance step by step. It takes a while to build a reputation and get good equipment, but you don't peak in the sport until age forty or so."

Women who want to begin a sport and who know that neither age nor risk should hold them back often encounter the objection that only certain sports are suitable for women beyond their teens. For example, adult swimming lessons are a standard at clubs and Ys everywhere, but a grown woman who has always yearned to go soaring from a high diving board will have a hard time finding anyone to teach her. Yet many women discover that they actually develop more nerve as they get older. A grandmother has set records in national speedboat racing, and a sixty-four-year-old retired schoolteacher I know recently tried scuba diving and parachute jumping.

During the past decade, housewives who had spent a dozen or more years at home with children began attending graduate schools and starting careers, and a rash of successful women in their late thirties have recently been switching professions and taking unexpected leaps to change their lives. "The same day I entered medical school I also moved to a new apartment, quit smoking, and began bicycling three miles a day," says a former nurse from Chicago who decided to start wearing the stethoscope when she was thirty-seven. Another woman, previously an administrative assistant for a large firm in New York, chose a similarly advanced age to enter Harvard Business School. "I was terrified," she says. "Talk about male bastions. I began playing squash every day with myself—just banging a ball around the court and pretending it was a male head. By the time I was good enough to challenge some of my classmates to a real game, a lot of my terror was gone."

A new awareness of physical competence doesn't always accompany a midlife efflorescence, but the two are linked often enough to be notable. When women become daring in sports they break through barriers and discover a new dimension in their lives.

Chapter Six

Choosing a Sport

Gå en tur med hunden, selv om du ingen har.
—Hjerteforeningen
(Take a walk with your dog, even if you don't have one.
—Danish Heart Association)

A college acquaintance whom I hadn't seen in a while met me
one day for an after-work drink, and once we had exchanged
a few cordialities, she took a sip of wine and got to the point.
"Here's the question every woman in Manhattan asks," she
said. "What do you do to keep in shape?" I mentioned that I
run a few miles by the East River every day—not as romantic
as it sounds since the running track is a cement sidewalk, barely
an arm's length from a major highway. She shook her head.
"I'm just not a runner," she said. She had been bored by exercise
classes at a club, weight machines weren't her style, and she
enjoyed swimming only in the ocean. "The only time I was
really happy about sports"—she sighed—"was when I was little
and played softball with the kids in my neighborhood. I loved
that game." Suddenly the prerequisite for staying in shape
seemed obvious. Keeping fit shouldn't be a chore; it can be a
happy side effect of having fun and feeling free. The tendency
to·think of fitness as something that is regulated and prepack-
aged changes the focus of activity from inspiring self-aware-
ness to drudging self-improvement. "I run two miles a day,"
says one teenager from Detroit, "and I hate it while I'm out
there. But I know men don't like flabby girls any more." This

do-it-and-be-done attitude doesn't work for long. It's hard to stick with an exercise regimen that's rewarding only when it's over. The actual physical benefits may be meager, too. Dr. George Sheehan, the sixty-year-old long-distance runner and philosopher, reports that studies of thirty thousand men in Ireland and England showed that coronary risk rates and heart disease were unaffected by jobs that involved hard physical labor. The heart attack rate did drop significantly, though, when the vigorous activity took place during leisure time. "Exercise that is work is worthless," concludes Sheehan. "But exercise that is play will give you health and long life."

Sheehan's claim may be excessive, but his instinct that sports should be a time for play is not. If sport is to be liberating, it must be approached with a sense of joy, not obligation. Most charts will claim that softball isn't as effective as, say, bicycling for improving endurance and strength; but in choosing a sport, there are factors more important than pulse rate and calories burned per hour. For example, Camille Lounds, an actress and former model who coaches fencing, insists that she began the sport to keep her body trim and lithe. Any number of activities would have done the same, but Camille was attracted to the Three Musketeers image of wielding a sword, or the modern equivalent, known as a foil. "When I pick up a foil, I take on the whole proud history of the sword—the romantic tradition of fighting for what you want and asserting yourself with grace," she says. Fencing is often called the physical equivalent of chess, since it's one sport where skill is more important than strength, and mental conditioning is vital. But the women who duel for their own honor are rarely overweight or out of shape. "You start noticing your body more when you're using it," says a fencer from Philadelphia, "and you just generally take better care of yourself." Fencing is a sport that you don't have to learn in the cradle, and many top fencers are in their twenties and thirties. Some who never picked up a foil until college have recently qualified for international teams. "I was a scrawny and gawky kid growing up in the shadow of an incredibly beautiful older sister," says Camille Lounds, a purposeful woman with hands and will of iron, "and fencing gave me a way to be special. I'm really putty under this veneer, but a sword gives you distinction. A sport should do more than just improve your looks."

What's the best way to choose a sport? In Russia, young people are given extensive personality tests, and the results are then matched by computer to the profiles of top athletes in a range of sports. That way, a physically talented but very sociable young girl doesn't get sent to a sports center where she'll spend hours involved in long-distance running. Taking a lesson from that, officials in this country adopted a pseudoscientific approach in selecting the first Junior Elite gymnasts—twenty youngsters chosen for a program meant to prep them for the Olympics. Though selected mostly on ability, they were interviewed, with their parents, to make sure they had a championship attitude. The family's physical traits were also investigated. "A ten-year-old can have a perfect gymnast's body," explains one of the officials of the U.S. Gymnastics Federation, "but if her parents are both six feet tall and heavy-boned, we'd know she might have a growth spurt and a very short career." And if one of the more talented girls should fit into that category? "We probably wouldn't eliminate her, anyway," admits the official. That's a reasonable decision. Enough athletes with questionable body types have succeeded in sports so that it's increasingly difficult to set standards, particularly for women. The famous line among basketball scouts is that a prospect "may be small, but he's quick." Before one girls' game, a coach announced her starting lineup to a group of reporters and gave a brief description of each player.

"Watch out for Julie at left guard," said the coach. "She's small, but she's also slow."

"Why the hell does she start?" asked a man from the local newspaper.

"Because she's got more wits than the rest of the team put together."

Jenni Chandler, a gum-chewing Southern belle who won an Olympic gold medal in diving when she was seventeen, thinks the only way to find a sport is to be forced into one. "When I was eight, my mama was chairman of our club's swim team. We didn't have any divers, so we were getting killed in all the meets. One day she dragged me over to the pool and made me start diving. I hated it." Jenni insists that she has also hated everything she's ever done when she first started. "I know you're not supposed to push kids, but if I have kids, I'm going to do a lot of pushing. Somebody has to make you get out and try. Like one day I was supposed to be learning a new dive from my coach, and when my dad drove me to the pool, I crouched on the floorboard of the car and wouldn't get out. He had to come around and physically carry me into the pool. I had a phobia about somersaults because I once did one off a rinky-dink diving board in someone's backyard and landed on my face. When I think about being scared of that now I just laugh. It was such an easy dive." But the lesson wasn't wasted. Shortly after the Olympics, her coach suggested that Jenni, the three-meter champion, should learn the tricks of the ten-meter board, too. "The high board scares me to death," she said with a sigh, "but I know what will happen. For a while I'll think about getting bruised or killed, then I'll get over the fear and really like it. Isn't it like that with everything in life?"

Being forced into a sport doesn't always have such a positive end, but often it's wise to try an activity that complements rather than reinforces normal patterns. "I love watching my girls blossom on the field," reports a junior high school soccer coach. "Most of the time they're worried about being sweet and popular, but when they're out there playing with people bashing into them, they stop being shy little girls. You can't be a pussycat when you have on cleats." One of the hardest tasks for most women is learning a sport that demands physical aggression. Martial-arts instructors report that they spend the first few lessons reminding women that it's all right to strike someone. "Intellectually they understand that, which is why they're taking the course in the first place," says a self-defense teacher in Los Angeles. "But you get a woman who has never expressed anger with her body and never hit anyone even playfully, and she has a real barrier to overcome." At one session, a delicate female student was working with the well-muscled male instructor, who outweighed her at least by half. He kept urging her to use more power, complaining that her weak chops and jabs were ineffective and lacked mettle. "I'm afraid of hurting you," she said at last, and although the comment brought peals of laughter from around the room, it was sincere.

Women manacle their power, afraid of the consequences of expressing themselves with their bodies. "Even when they're being attacked, women don't have permission to defend themselves," says Ann McAllister, a psychologist who directs a Rape Crisis Center in Atlanta. "I see this over and over with rape victims who are too scared to fight back, even when they'd have a chance. They become paralyzed because they have no sense of their physical competence." Dr. McAllister insists that women should be taught how to take care of themselves and protect themselves so that they don't give up too quickly in any situation that demands physical expression. "Most women want to be able to let go, but they need encouragement on the first step," says Dr. McAllister. A variety of activities including team sports and the martial arts can help with that. Julia Jones, an elderly woman who is in the fencing Hall of Fame and coaches at Hunter College in New York, thinks her sport also helps women get rid of their old bugaboos. "Girls are very timid when they start because they're afraid of hitting anybody," she says. "Fencing is good for them because it helps them get rid of their inhibitions. After a while, they're not so afraid of anything and they've really sharpened their wits."

It's important for women to get involved in activities in which they can take the initiative rather than holding back and simply reacting. Girls channeled into pep squads and cheerleading teams may be exercising their bodies, but the total experience is sorely wanting. Joan Lind, a rower from California, remembers that in high school she was a pepster—"You know, a rah-rah girl"—and thoroughly devoted herself to it. When she began rowing in college, she assumed that it would be much the same kind of activity—just something else to work on perfecting after school. "It didn't occur to me that it was a totally different experience until I entered my first big race," she says. "I was preparing to launch, and my coach leaned over and said that if I did well, my whole outlook on myself would change. And it did. I could have been the best pepster in the school, and I would never have felt that surge of achievement. What's nice about a sport like rowing is that everything's clear-cut, and there's a kind of challenge you don't have in normal life. You know what you have to accomplish, and you either go out there and do it, or not." Joan began rowing for recreation when some women she knew invited her to join them at the Long Beach boathouse. After about two days she wanted to give up, but her friends expected her to appear at the lake every morning. Finally she was too enraptured to quit. "Your motivations change after a while," she says. "For a long time I just wanted to see what I could do, and every day I wondered how much more I'd improve. After a certain level of training, you're pushing beyond pain barriers, and it turns into a spite thing—you've worked too hard to let anybody beat you now. I don't think of myself as a superaggressive person, but I was aggressive in training. Maybe that's why I loved it so much. I was finding a whole new side of myself. There was an intensity which I'd never experienced before."

That intensity is often hard to find. The stretching and flexibility routines which usually make up the major part of the "ladies'" programs at places like hotel gyms and European health spas and two-for-the-price-of-one exercise classes are the easiest but least beneficial kinds of exercises for most women. Stretching makes a muscle relax and increases agility, but it does nothing for strength or toning. The basic aim of a good exercise program should be to discipline the muscles, which requires making them work.

There are dozens of ways to categorize sports, and exercises are sometimes divided into isometric, isokinetic, and aerobic. Isometrics involves contracting a muscle in a static position—arm wrestling, for example, or pushing for a few seconds against any resisting object. Equipment like the Bullworker is often advertised on the back pages of men's magazines as a get-strong-quick isometric trick which can develop bulk in men and make specific muscles stronger. Isokinetic exercises are generally more valuable since they involve resistance (which builds strength) through a whole range of motion. Activities from scrubbing a wall to doing push-ups are isokinetic and build muscle tone and strength. Aerobics are generally hailed as the only "total" exercises, since they condition the cardiovascular system. But much of this categorizing can be misleading. For example, swimming is usually considered a total exercise, even though it's quite possible to stroke lazily across a pool and barely get the heart stirred. And while weight lifting is often criticized as an exercise for the muscles that does nothing for general fitness, that's not necessarily true. A vigorous program of weight training can get the heart beating to 70 percent of capacity—which is the ideal level for health-inducing exercises. Nearly all sports develop motor coordination, and most "ball" sports require hand-eye coordination, which girls without sports training often lack—but can acquire. "Skill usually transfers from one sport to another," says a young woman who played on three varsity teams in college. "Your reaction time and quickness get developed in, say, tennis, so you're that much better the next season when you try playing basketball." The point is that the best way to choose a sport is to find something that's fun and available. Rather than becoming involved exclusively in aerobic sports, find any activity and do it aerobically —with vigor and intensity.

Women often begin exercising to lose weight and so choose a sport which promises to use up the most calories. This can be deceptive. Diet books are fond of pointing out that a calorie is a calorie; it can be gained through a carrot stick or chocolate bar and used up while sleeping (about 60 calories per hour) or running (more than 500). But the value of an activity can't be judged by calorie charts alone. For example, depending on your weight, your body needs roughly 100 calories to move one mile. Whether you do that through thirty minutes of walking or seven minutes of running doesn't really matter to the calorie count—but the benefits of the run are far greater. Unless a walk is vigorous enough to raise the heart rate considerably, it doesn't change the level at which your body is operating. A short run puts new strain on all the muscles and makes the heart and lungs work harder. Eventually, the heart gets stronger, so that it sends out more blood with each stroke, and daily blood pressure and pulse rate will drop.

Finding What Fits

Sports doctors often insist that the bodies of endomorphs, ectomorphs, and mesomorphs are suited to different sports. But unless one is aiming for Olympic recognition, it's nonsensical to stay away from an activity that intrigues you because you feel physically inadequate. Often the suspected shortcoming exists only when the sport is defined in men's terms (a woman football player doesn't have to weigh 200 pounds—or even 150) or is based on an invalid premise. For example, most of the best women golfers are compact rather than lanky, but Carol Mann, consistently one of the top players on the women's professional tour, is 6'3". At one tournament, a reporter noticed her towering over the rest of the women and asked how a woman of her height had dared to take up golf. She stared at him briefly. "Well, I was too tall to make the chess team in my high school, so I tried golf." He looked bewildered for a moment, and hurried away.

Often an athlete's most valuable asset has nothing to do with physical type or natural ability. "When somebody has been given good exposure to a sport, great coaching, and opportunities for participating, she can capitalize on the least bit of talent," says Dr. John Marshall. "We can give guidelines, but I'd never say someone *shouldn't* participate in an activity. For example, Chris Evert is a very loose individual, and if I were profiling her, not knowing who she was, I'd say that she wouldn't be very good at explosive sports—like tennis."

Obviously, considerations of averages shouldn't prevent anyone from pursuing a sport that especially appeals, but there are factors to ponder before beginning. Knowing how your body is made is important in finding a sport in which (1) you can do well, and (2) you won't get hurt. It's particularly important to know whether you're loose or tight, so you can then consider what the new sport demands and what you should do to prepare yourself. If you lack flexibility but plan to try diving or judo, you should be stretching the muscles and joints. Dr. James Nicholas recommends "segmental stretching"—that is, stretching each muscle group separately and gently. Someone who is very tight and worried about muscle pulls or hurting her lower back might try doing stretching exercises in a swimming pool or lake. The buoyancy from the water removes much of the strain.

Don't give up on a sport just because of body type. Linda Fratianne has succeeded in ice-skating even though she is a tight-jointed woman in a sport where flexibility and agility count for a good deal. Relying on power and control, she was one of the first women in the world to do a triple jump, but she also goes to a ballet class at least twice a week for stretching exercises. "Whenever we're in a strange city, my mother goes to the hotel clerk right away and asks for a dance teacher," she says. "I need someone who can stretch me out; otherwise I'm so stiff I can't do anything." Before she won her world championship in Tokyo in 1977, Linda was "stretched" by a Japanese ballet master who didn't speak a word of English but smiled and bowed as he prepared Linda to perform.

A flexible woman who has never been very active before and wants to take up something like soccer should have no qualms; but she should prepare herself with some leg-strengthening exercises and be careful about getting good equipment, even to start. Beyond that, elaborate preparations are unnecessary and are often excuses rather than precautions. Usually the best way to learn a sport is to go out and do it. Be willing to feel clumsy for a few days, but actually pick up the racket, ball, or bat and start using the muscles the sport requires. Sports played in an enclosed court—such as racquetball or squash—are great since even beginners can have fun. Unlike the neophyte tennis player, you don't have the frustration of trying to get the ball over the net, and you don't spend half your time shagging mis-hit balls. After an hour or so, you can have enjoyable rallies, even if you lack style. "Too many people get hung up on learning the basics when they'd actually do better to just plunge right into the sport," says Dr. Laurence Morehouse, director of the Human Performance Laboratory at UCLA. "For an adult, it's really not necessary to crawl before you can run. After all, the two involve very different motions."

Women often forget that being oversized and brawny isn't necessary for involvement in sports. When I appeared on a television talk show once, the hostess, whom I hadn't yet met, introduced me as a sportswriter, then looked startled when I walked on the set. "Since you write about jocks, I somehow expected you to be much bigger," she said. I wanted to explain that writing doesn't build muscles, but I didn't bother, since women involved in sports—as reporters, participants, or champs—invariably get that reaction. I was guilty of similar prejudging when I first met Diana Nyad, the marathon swimmer, whom I expected to be big, with broad shoulders and massive legs. Instead, she turned out to be about my size—a humbling discovery, since there was no obvious reason for her athletic superiority. The stereotype that athletes must be musclebound may be unconsciously maintained by some women as an excuse for fragility and ineptness at sports. But it's generally unfair. When Dr. Nicholas evaluated the factors that contribute to successful sports performance, body type was only one of the twenty-one variables he cited. Others included alertness, motivation, coordination, balance, and discipline. Until she gradu-ated from Delta State in 1978, Debbie Brock was one of the best women basketball players in the country, even though she is only 4'11" tall. She was one of the stars on the team when Delta State won its national championships, and she could always cause hilarity in a locker room by stepping into the sneakers of a 6'4" teammate and flopping around like a clown. How did such a little girl dare to enter a Brobdingnagian's sport? "I never thought of myself as small," she said to me once, "and I like to play, so I do."

According to Dr. Nicholas's evaluation, there are only four sports in which body type actually is very important: basketball (though Debbie doesn't believe that), football, jockey riding, and ballet. In the latter two, being small is a requirement, but even that is changing. When Cynthia Gregory, one of the prin-cipal dancers with the American Ballet Theatre, balances on point, she's six feet of power. Rudolph Nureyev calls her the best dancer in America, but when she first arrived in New York at the age of nineteen, the directors of the ABT insisted that she was too tall to be a ballerina. "They thought anyone over five foot two was a giant," she says. Cynthia's elegantly propor-tioned body convinced the critics that a ballerina doesn't have to be a wisp of gossamer. "You also don't have to start with a perfect body," says Cynthia. "It's amazing the ugly bodies some dancers have overcome through training. For example, dancers don't all have a naturally long neck—we get them from carrying ourselves perfectly erect."

Edward Villella, a dancer with the New York City Ballet, choreographed and appeared in a film called "The Dance of the Athlete," which appeared several times on television. Villella wanted to show that dance and sports use many of the same movements and that a six-minute pas de deux may require more strength than four rounds of boxing. (Villella has grounds for comparing, since he was once a welterweight boxing cham-pion.) It may seem that the graceful and ethereal ballerinas never sweat or grunt, but they actually have tough, sinewy muscles and tremendous stamina. Other women who struggled for years in pink tutus will find that childhood ballet lessons are a good background for several sports. Many ballet movements, from the grand jeté to the arabesque, are paralleled in tennis and other racquet games; fencing uses lunge movements and pliés; basketball and volleyball mimic the jumps and leg extensions of ballet; and soccer requires balancing and kicks. "I suppose I should call my mother and thank her for making me go to ballet school," says a woman who plays on her college soccer team. "I don't think this is what she had in mind when she said ballet would make me a girl, but now we've both gotten our way."

Time, Weather, and Inclination

A girl who's exposed to a variety of sports early will invariably stumble on the sport that suits her needs and physical abilities —just as a boy can usually announce by age six that he detests baseball, loves lacrosse, and is no good at swimming. But women in their twenties and thirties who are entering the sports world for the first time since hopscotch days may give some extra thought to finding the right sport, one that can be easily and regularly pursued and isn't done grudgingly. When a young woman named Sandy moved from suburban Florida to downtown Chicago, she joined a YWCA so that she could keep up her swimming—now in a four-lane pool rather than an ocean. After a few weeks, her daily swim had turned into a twice-weekly swim, and eventually even that felt like a burden. "I hated going there," says Sandy. "I like swimming outside, I don't like chlorine, and I can never keep in a lane. I was still calling myself a swimmer, but when my membership in the Y ran out, I realized how little I'd used it." Sandy eventually decided that swimming would have to be her vacation sport and chose squash as a more suitable city game.

A few sports, like golf and downhill skiing, aren't much fun unless you take the time to develop a degree of skill. Golf and skiing also demand an investment of money, for equipment, fees, and lessons. While many cities have well-tended public courses, golf is still largely a country-club sport and membership fees can be high. Finding a club that doesn't discriminate against women is a challenge in itself. Many restrict the hours when women can play and reserve weekend tee-off times for men, despite the fact that women may work all day and pay the same club dues as the men. (Women in Canada have the Ladies' Golf Club of Toronto, probably the only club right now that is owned by women and has an exclusively female membership. Men are allowed to play as guests.) A few tennis clubs also segregate the men and women. Writer Lois Gould once said that she spends every summer planning to take up tennis, just so she can protest the unfair rules at her local club. It's possible to play and enjoy tennis even if your skills aren't finely honed, but golf is generally more frustrating for a novice. And it isn't practical for women on tight schedules, because even the quickest round of golf takes about two hours.

For women who live in a city, downhill skiing, like golf or scuba diving, is a weekend get-away sport. With the new teaching methods, you can learn to negotiate a hill quickly and might be snowplowing down a mountain by the end of a weekend. But if you have no patience for ski-lift lines and expensive instruction, cross-country skiing is a good alternative. You can rent the skis for a small amount or fully equip yourself for about $100. On wintry days, while the downhill skiers are planning vacations in Sun Valley or Aspen or Stowe, the cross-country devotees don't have to wait. "I learned to cross-country ski in Central Park," says one New York woman, "and on a very snowy day it's a beautiful place to go. One whole week during the blizzard last year, I walked to work every morning on skis, cutting through the park. There were a lot of people doing that, and everyone was very friendly." In one Swedish study, female cross-country skiers were found to have the best aerobic capacity of any of the women tested. Enthusiasts of the sport say it's as easy as walking. It's not, but after a day or so of tripping over tangled skis, you can proceed smoothly. Cross-country skiers who don't have time to escape to the country for woodsy solitude often appear at the lakefront in Chicago or even on the streets of St. Paul, Minnesota. Any golf course, public or private, is a haven for the cross-country skier who wants to stay near home. In the winter, there's nobody around to ban women from the course during peak hours.

Even if you detest cold weather, you can be active outdoors during the winter without much discomfort. When you're running, cross-country skiing, skating, or playing soccer, your body is generating so much heat that all your clothes have to do is maintain it. During winter races, competitors generally cross the finish line soaked in sweat. I'm normally very susceptible to the cold (I keep a quilt *and* an electric blanket on my bed), but I've never had any problem running outside, even during cold New England winters. I rely on layers: tights, knee socks, shorts, and sweatpants; a turtleneck shirt, pullover sweater, and warm-up jacket; wool gloves topped with mittens; and a wool hat. But if you've spent your whole life in Palm Springs and can't bear stepping outside during the winter now that you've moved to Maine, an indoor sport like racquetball or squash may be a good compromise. A young woman from Anchorage, Alaska, told me that she stays in shape during the bleakest months by running up and down the stairs in her ten-story apartment house several times a day. Worries about weather and illness are usually poor excuses rather than reasons for quitting a sport. At Stanford, the women swim year round in the outdoor pool, even though Palo Alto winters can get chilly. "I was always complaining about freezing, but I didn't have a cold the whole time I was swimming on the team," says one female graduate. "Lately I haven't been swimming and I've been getting sick all the time. I've heard a lot of people say the same thing. I guess when your body is used to changes in temperature, your resistance is high." An interesting scene occurs in the skating clubs of Southern California, where many young girls spend hours every day in the cold indoor rinks, practicing spins and figure eights and dreaming about national competitions. In the early afternoons, the parking lots are filled with mothers unloading youngsters, blankets, and down parkas from their station wagons. It could pass for a scene at a Harvard-Yale football game in November, but it regularly occurs under the searing sun and ninety-five-degree temperature of a July day. Climate shouldn't deter you from any sport.

Many women athletes have chosen their sports through happenstance. When Billie Jean King was a youngster her first love was softball, but since there weren't any professional opportunities for girls in that sport, she started tennis. Sometimes playing what's popular is a good idea, since better coaching and more facilities are available. In the fifties, the weekday-morning ladies leagues made bowling a prime sport; and in the late sixties, the surge was in tennis, with its fifty-dollar-per-hour rates at some private clubs and long waits at public courts. The shift in the mid-seventies brought in the individualistic running fad. Right now, young women in northern Texas are playing soccer, those in St. Louis and Detroit are choosing racquetball, and many in Southern California are trying roller-skating. The newest games seem to provide a compromise between sport as exercise and sport as enjoyment.

It takes a certain amount of nerve to start playing a sport that you've never tried before. One young woman recalls attending an organizational meeting for an incipient women's ice hockey team when she was an undergraduate at Princeton. "I loved the idea of playing, but I'd never been on hockey skates in my life and I didn't know how I could fit the practices into my schedule. Besides, I'm not much of an athlete, and I figured I'd be cut the second day—so I just left the meeting and decided I wasn't meant to be on the team. Later on I got to know some of the women who stuck it out. Not one of them had ever worn hockey skates before that year. Frankly, it was a little embarrassing to realize that the real reason I didn't play was lack of confidence. Actually, it was more like sheer terror at trying something that foreign to me. You can bet I regret that now."

Sometimes it's easier to begin two sports than one. The rewards are certainly more than double, since the activities will complement each other. If you begin a gymnastics class, your grace and agility will likely improve, and you'll achieve some degree of skill at tumbling moves. But if you also bicycle a few miles every day, you'll progress much faster. Bicycling increases aerobic power and leg strength. Better endurance makes it easier to last through a gymnastics routine, and added leg power means flips and somersaults can be done with new buoyancy and less strain on the arms. Different parts of the body don't work discretely. When muscle power throughout the body isn't coordinated, your progress in any activity will be impeded, and there's a greater risk of injury. Dr. LeRoy Perry, a sports chiropractor, recommends body-balancing techniques. "Unilateral anything is a state of disease," he says. "It's like a bow and arrow. You make the string too tight and the bow bends. You make the muscles on one side strong, and the weak ones on the other side are going to pull or be out of place. Proper balance is everything." He urges right-handed baseball pitchers to warm up by first going through the pitching motion left-handed, and suggests that golfers and tennis players also practice the motions of their sports from both sides. Similarly, you can keep your body working cohesively by counterpoising the advantages of one sport with those of another. For example, running five days a week on a hard surface will strengthen the cardiovascular system and make legs and hips firmer, but it also causes knots in the leg muscles and tightness in the lower back. It's wiser to run three times a week and offset any negative results with two days of swimming, which stretches the muscles and encourages a wide range of motion.

One dash of caution: Exercise works quickly, but the body does require a brief period of transition from its old habits to the new effervescence. If you're still exhausted more than an hour after a workout, you're probably pushing too hard. Be nicer to yourself, but don't quit. A woman named Diane who was completing a Ph.D. thesis complained to friends that she was feeling slothful and flabby from spending hours translating texts in a library cubicle. They convinced her to swim with them in the evenings, but after a week, she quit. "I'd come home from the pool and fall asleep," she says. "I decided that it was either get in shape or get my Ph.D." Her swim chums couldn't understand her defection, since they always felt recharged after their laps. Diane probably needed an additional week or two for her body to become accustomed to the increased load, and at that point, she would have felt her energy and spirits lifting. The worst part of any sports program is the first week.

By choosing a sport that you can play without a great deal of inconvenience and that's more or less suited to your body type and inclinations, you're making it likely that you'll feel good about your sport—and yourself—pretty quickly.

Chapter Seven

Nutrition, Diets, and Secret Potions

*How can one play and think and find truth when stuffed
with jelly doughnuts?*
—*George Sheehan*

Women looking for the extra something that will give them
more energy often look in the refrigerator. Some athletes seem
to spend more time planning their meals than they do training.
As they become more conscious of their bodies, most women
find that eating to lose weight is less important than eating for
fitness. Athletic women tend to have a different attitude toward
food than do those who wonder only what lunch will do to
their hips. Since there's a growing conviction that what goes
into the body has a direct effect on athletic performance, they're
always looking for the food, pill, or potion that will bring a gold
medal. Food fads pass quickly among women athletes, who are
usually willing to try anything from mung beans to goat's
cheese if it will help them do better. But an athlete who finds
a good-for-you food that seems to work can turn fanatical. One
runner almost caused an international incident when she asked
her Russian hosts at a track meet to give her wheat germ for
breakfast and they gave her something resembling Wheaties.
She mumbled a few words about sabotage, turned the offending
bowl upside down, and stalked out of the room. This story was
told to me with some amusement the next year, since by then
wheat germ had passed from fashion and the runner's new

prerace miracle was French toast with gobs of strawberry jelly.

Many athletes' diets are based on absolutely no medical facts, but most coaches agree that if a player *thinks* she'll do better by eating a certain food, she probably will. Swimmer Debbie Meyer is fond of peanut butter and used to eat dollops of it before going into the water. After she won one of her Olympic gold medals, someone sent her a bouquet of flowers with a jar of Skippy in the middle. Dick Buerkle, a small, bald man who at thirty began breaking track records and ran the mile faster than anyone in the world, has the same passion as Debbie and says he owes his success to peanut butter sandwiches. "He thinks peanut butter is the perfect food," reports his wife.

The most typical sports diet seems to be based on avoiding white sugar and white flour and eating very little meat. Raw fruits and vegetables are mainstays for many athletes, and increased numbers of them have become vegetarians, their credo being that you don't have to eat muscles to get them. When basketball player Bill Walton decided one year that he needed to gain weight, he did what any reasonable person would: He began to eat more. For a few months he stuffed himself with sunflower seeds, vegetables, and nuts, and by the time the season started, he had gained forty pounds and enough strength to lead his team, the Portland Trailblazers, to the National Basketball Association championship. Walton is a strict vegetarian (he won't even eat milk products or eggs), and one reporter wryly noted that it was time to change the standard sports metaphors, since Walton clearly could not be strong as an ox.

Athletic women who have become vegetarians insist that they feel better, are less logy, and are just as powerful as when they ate meat. When Dr. Joan Ullyot analyzed the blood chemistries of a cross section of the population, she concluded that the healthiest people are vegetarian athletes. They're followed by inactive vegetarians, then athletes on ordinary diets. Inactive types on ordinary diets are at the bottom of the list; their blood-fat and cholesterol levels are almost always too high.

The positive effects of exercise and meatless diets in preventing heart disease are becoming increasingly well documented. Like Joan Ullyot, Dr. Peter Wood, a professor and researcher at Stanford University, has found that cholesterol levels are substantially lower in athletes than in inactive people. Possibly more important, he has also found that the distribution of the cholesterol is noticeably different among the active. Cholesterol is carried in the blood by lipoproteins of two types: high density and low density. From his research, Dr. Wood has conjectured that high levels of the high-density particles protect against heart attacks. In various studies, Dr. Wood has found that the ratio of high- to low-density particles is generally twice as great in women athletes as among a control group. Checking for triglycerides—the other major fatty substance in the blood that has been connected with heart disease—Dr. Wood found that the levels in athletes were 50 percent lower than for nonathletes, meaning that the athletes' risk of heart disease is considerably less.

When analyses are done solely on the basis of diet, vegetarians (whatever their activity levels) have considerably lower blood pressures and fat levels than comparable groups of meat-eaters. A government study of 100,000 Seventh-Day Adventists (who eat eggs and dairy products but no meats) revealed that their incidence of heart disease is 40 percent lower than is typical among Americans, and their incidence of cancer is half the typical rate. Other studies have linked the incidence of cancers of the colon and breast to diets high in animal fat. For women, vegetarian diets may have still another important effect; the Environmental Protection Agency has found that the level of pesticides in the breast milk of vegetarian women is about one-half that of women on a conventional diet.

Some athletes in grueling sports—generally marathon running and occasionally rugby or soccer—rely on "carbohydrate loading" before an important event. Carbohydrates turn into glycogen, the substance that keeps the muscles working. Normally, the body has enough glycogen stored for about two hours of continuous hard work, such as running nonstop. After that, the glycogen supply has been consumed and the body finds it difficult to continue. The point of carbohydrate loading is to get an extra supply of glycogen stored in the muscles. It's done by first depleting glycogen by training hard (to use up whatever is present) and spending about three days on a strict protein diet. Then, two or three days before a big race or game, carbohydrates are restored to the diet, and it's all right to eat as much pasta and nonwhite bread and fruit as feels good. The initial deprivation causes the body to overcompensate when carbohydrates are again available and store more glycogen than normal. One interesting note is that many athletes stay away from this procedure because they become too unbearably weak on the high-protein days. For active women, a no-carbohydrate diet is not a good idea.

One source of carbohydrates that most athletes consume regularly is beer. Before his second fight with Muhammad Ali, heavyweight boxing champion Leon Spinks was fueling himself with meals of raw eggs and two bottles of beer. He claimed that the beer didn't mean he was breaking training but was simply his way of replenishing the salt he lost sparring. Other athletes suggest that a glass of beer before or after strenuous exercise will prevent cramps by blocking lactic acid buildup in the muscles. Twelve-year-old runner Laura Craven has convinced her mother that a glass of beer after a race eases her pains, and the night before Frank Shorter won the gold medal in the Olympic marathon, he drank about a six pack of beer to relax. The next morning he swallowed a Danish and four or five cups of coffee to get hyped up again. "I don't use any drugs other than caffeine and alcohol because I like to maintain a reasonable amount of control over my body," he says. "If you take any of the stronger drugs—like any kind of speed—your reactions can really get out of hand." Shorter drinks defizzed Coke or Pepsi while he's running a marathon. "Your physiological and mental cycles go up and down during a race," he says. "Caffeine gives you a jolt that can help you out of a lull." Many athletes shun caffeine during or before an event, however, insisting it gives them diarrhea or stomach spasms. For some reason, constipation is almost never a problem for an active person. Members of the Ex-Lax crowd are generally victims of a sedentary life-style, and exercise may work better than store-bought medicine to alleviate their problem. Sometimes exercise causes the opposite difficulty. Dr. Jack Scaff, who leads the running clinics in Kapiolani Park in Honolulu, notes that "it's common to get the trots from trotting." If cutting caffeine intake doesn't help, sometimes eliminating whole milk will. Before it can be absorbed in the body, milk must be broken down by an enzyme called lactase, and the enzyme may diminish as people get older, causing an intolerance to milk. Often the problem is mild enough not to be noticed except during exercise, when the milk sugar becomes a major irritant. Other dairy products like cheese and yogurt won't necessarily affect the body in the same way, since enzymes may be added or changed during the processing of these products.

Cramps during or after exercise are sometimes the result of dehydration, so it's important to sip water or unsweetened juice often while playing, particularly on very hot or humid days. Some coaches dispense salt tablets regularly during summer workouts, to replace sodium lost through perspiration, but the tablets are often a bad idea. They can irritate the stomach lining, since they may take a long time to dissolve, and they may contribute to a bloated feeling that won't arise from water alone. An overabundance of salt (or sodium) is unhealthy for the kidneys and heart and can cause dehydration, since the body drains water from its vital organs in an effort to flush the sodium out of the system. Potassium works like sodium in regulating the system's fluid balance, and it also helps nourish the muscles. So, instead of eating salty foods like pretzels and potato chips, it's reasonable to rely on foods high in potassium like bananas and tomatoes to prevent cramps.

The various thirst-quenching drinks marketed for athletes are of dubious value. The most popular, Gatorade, is sweet and contains far less potassium than a glass of milk, beer, or orange juice. Sugar slows down the absorption of fluid from the stomach, so in an activity where fluid is being lost quickly (like long-distance running or rugby), Gatorade will be less efficient at preventing dehydration of the muscles and tissues than a glass of plain water. Another common drink, ERG, was developed by a chemist and runner named Bill Gookin who claims he analyzed his own sweat to find out exactly what was being lost and created his concoction—Electrolyte Replacement with Glucose—as the perfect restorative. Because of the glucose, it has the same limitations as the sugary Gatorade, and in any event, the magic formula is probably unnecessary. All that needs to be replaced immediately after exercise is fluid, since whatever nutrients are lost will be replenished in a normal diet. If a good deal of salt is being lost through sweat, the kidneys will compensate by not releasing as much salt in the urine. A salad with leafy vegetables and tomatoes will put back the minerals depleted by exercise, but you should choose your greens carefully. Iceberg lettuce has about the same nutritional content as tissue paper; raw spinach or other kinds of lettuce like Bib, Boston, and romaine (or cos) are far better.

Sugar not only slows down the absorption of fluids, it represses the secretion of gastric juices—which means that foods eaten with sugar sit in the stomach longer, causing acidity and often an accumulation of gas. When meat and sugar are eaten together—say, a hamburger with a Coke—acid fermentation will generally occur in the stomach. William Dufty, the author of *Sugar Blues*, writes that in the presence of sugar, animal protein may rot in the stomach before it is even converted into usable amino acids. "When proteins are taken with sugar, they putrefy, they are broken down into a variety of ptomaines and leucomaines, which are nonusable substances—poisons," he writes.[1] Dufty notes that after a person has eaten something heavy, like red meat, the body may crave to balance it with

1. William Dufty, *Sugar Blues* (New York: Warner Books, 1975), p. 163.

something light and sweet. Getting protein from fish or vegetables keeps the system more stabilized and makes it easier to avoid these swings. When sugar is refined, nearly all the vitamins and minerals are removed. Substituting brown sugar isn't much help, since that's often just refined sugar to which molasses has been added. Raw sugar is supposed to be unrefined, but if you read the labels on some packages, you discover that much of it is refined sugar which has been crystallized for a "natural" look.

In listing nutritional content, package labels don't distinguish between natural and refined carbohydrates. But the Federal Trade Commission has ruled that refined sugar can't be referred to as a "nutrient" or "energy builder" in advertisements, and a report from the American Medical Association calls refined sugar an *anti*-nutrient, since it has none of its own nutrients and draws on the body's supply of B vitamins to be metabolized.

There is a similar problem with refined grain. Most flour comes from a wheat kernel, which has three layers: the outer layer or bran; the germ; and the endosperm, or starchy inner core. The bran and germ contain the vitamins and minerals, but they are more coarsely textured and spoil more easily than the endosperm. Commercial producers who want a uniform product use only the endosperm. The white flour which emerges from their mills is finely textured, fluffy, and as nutritious as Elmer's Glue. To make up for what has been left on the mill floor, synthetic vitamins are added, and the packagers boast that the flour is "enriched" or "fortified." A processed cold cereal is nutritious, according to the information on the side panel, but what's inside is something like cardboard doused with vitamin pills. Debate on the comparative value of synthetic and natural vitamins continues, but if you prefer to get your nutrients in natural form, try raw wheat germ.

Women athletes have been quick to kick the sugar habit. Billie Jean King, who once happily referred to herself as a junk-food addict, now barely glances at cakes and cookies. When tennis player Martina Navratilova first defected to the United

States from Czechoslavakia, she talked delightedly about the joys of America: ice cream, cookies, and hot dogs. At that point, she was a stocky, strong, and potentially great tennis player who liked to eat. Within the next few years, winning became more important than gorging to her; Martina turned to salads and fruits and dropped about twenty pounds. She didn't lose an ounce of strength and gained considerable quickness. By 1978 she was devouring the Virginia Slims tennis tour and became the leading money winner on the circuit, accumulating over $200,000 in the first three months of the year. "Martina decided that cars and diamonds are just as patriotic as pizza," said one of her friends. That same year, another standout on the circuit, Kerry Melville Reid, lost twenty pounds and "dropped below a hundred and thirty for the first time in as long as I can remember." She claimed that being lighter and more fit was the best protection against injury.

In sports like boxing, wrestling, and crew, athletes are always trying to drop enough pounds to compete in a lower weight division. I once spent a week observing a male wrestler who weighed about 170 pounds and was living on Jell-O and vitamin pills for several days, trying to "make weight." The day before his match he was still six pounds overweight, so he sat in a steam room, then ran several miles in a sweatsuit. The next morning he hit the scales at 150 pounds. When I expressed awe at the amazing poundage change, he insisted that everyone on the team did just about the same every week. After the match, win or lose, they would all have an eating orgy with pizzas, gallons of ice cream, and grain-alcohol punch. Monday it was back to Jell-O.

The wrestlers on their crash diets are losing water weight and very little else. It may take thirty-five miles of running to lose a pound of flesh, but a pound of water will drain off in about two miles. Until recently, women athletes have been spared the quick-loss traumas, since there haven't been enough competitors to warrant weight divisions in events. But that's beginning to change, and women aren't always more reasonable than men in planning sensible diets. Since a low weight can lead to extra mounts, jockey Robyn Smith is compulsive about maintaining her lean and hungry look. "In the mornings I have yogurt and wheat germ, and at night I have a salad and maybe a little meat," she says. "Occasionally I have white wine." But Robyn suspends her starvation plan now and then for incredible eating binges. Writer Frank Deford, a companion at one of these meals, reported that Robyn devoured two shrimp cocktails, a steak, two orders of prime ribs, and a huge salad before leaving the table. The next day she returned righteously to small orders of food and large orders of diet pills. Ballet dancers are similarly notorious for wicked diets—they nibble lettuce, drink coffee, and puff cigarettes to stay away from food. One ballerina tried living on licorice for a while, since she had heard that it passed through the system quickly and caused loose bowels. "You don't get fat if nothing stays in your body very long," she said solemnly. Because they don't want to feel heavy on stage, ballerinas tend to eat only one meal a day, after the evening performance. A notable exception is Patricia McBride, one of the stars of the New York City Ballet. She loves pasta with meat and will sit down to a big plate of it about two hours before she dances.

How much to eat before exercising—and, indeed, whether or not to eat at all—is difficult to prescribe. Dr. Ernest van Aaken, the godfather of women's distance running, recommends a Spartan diet for athletes. His philosophy is: Run hungry. He figures nobody ever got fast from food. When the editors of *Runner's World* magazine surveyed competitors at a 20-kilometer race in Chicago, they found that the best athletes generally ate nothing, or very little, before running. If the blood is being used for digestion, it can't be pouring into the heart, lungs, and muscles, where it's most needed during a race. Some coaches discount this theory. "Girls are used to starving themselves to be model-thin, and they don't realize how much energy they could have if they ate properly," says a basketball coach from Florida. "I'm not in favor of excess weight, but some of the girls want to get so skinny that they can't maintain good health—let alone develop strength."

Weight and power don't always correlate. Nancy Lopez, the golfer who began smashing records on the pro tour as a twenty-one-year-old rookie, recalls that when she was a skinny kid growing up in Rosewell, New Mexico, her father was always insisting, "Ten more pounds, ten more yards." "But it doesn't work that way," Nancy told me grimly one morning as she stared at a breakfast of bran flakes, skim milk, and orange juice. "When I was a senior in high school I gained thirty pounds, and I wasn't hitting the ball thirty yards farther." By the next year, too many chiliburgers and meals at McDonald's had driven her weight up to 170 pounds (Nancy is only 5'4" tall), and despite a series of quick-loss diets, she was still overweight when she turned professional. "I finally went on a reasonable diet then," she says, "because I realized that being in shape helps my timing and helps me to swing better. I also feel proud of myself, and instead of walking down the fairway looking all heavy, I have a lot more confidence." Her plan for losing weight slowly and consistently: breakfast as always, only smaller portions and no bacon or sausage; a light salad for lunch so that she won't be playing on a full stomach; and dinner of fish or chicken and vegetables, eaten early—"so I can digest it, and maybe even burn some of the calories, before bed." While she was losing weight, Nancy won more prize money than any rookie golfer —male or female—ever before.

Often, looking good and feeling good coincide. Diving coach Ron O'Brien helps his athletes find a weight at which they can look sleek plunging into the water but still be able to do their most challenging dives after a whole day of competition. "At one time or another, all of us divers pork out," says champion Jenni Chandler. "Once four of us were training at Fort Lauderdale with Ron, and he humiliated us with weigh-ins every Monday. We had really gotten blimpy-looking, but we lost the fat fast enough on low-carbohydrate diets. I thought we should tease Ron, so three of us kept losing weight until we were way under and he got mad at us for *that.* It was a kick." Ron had a hard time getting angry at Jenni's prank. "I guess it's good when girls can have fun with themselves and not get hysterical over pounds," he shrugs. Billie Moore, the coach of the UCLA women's basketball team, also requires Monday weight checks. "I stress quickness with my team and keep the women very weight conscious," she says. "Anybody who doesn't think five pounds makes any difference should go get a five-pound weight and try running with it. That's the extra burden you carry around when you weigh too much." Coach Moore doesn't give her athletes special diets, though, and even shuns the traditional team training meal before most games. "Everyone thrives on different foods," she says, "and once a woman has been in shape and knows how her body *should* feel, she can find the best diet for herself."

It's easy to overestimate the number of calories necessary for normal athletic activities, and the stoking some women do before going out to run or play tennis may be comforting but unnecessary. A woman in her late twenties named Amy remembers that when she first began playing squash, she would devour bananas and candy for about an hour before heading to the court. "I'd be thinking about the game, and I'd get panicked," she says. "I always figured that I wasn't really strong enough to last a whole match, and I had to do something so that I wouldn't end up lying on the court and panting." Another woman liked to swallow raisins before a tennis match. "I knew vaguely about the connections between iron and oxygen supply," she says, "and I had an image of the raisins coming to my rescue when I was about to miss a cross-court backhand at game point."

Sometimes painfully little attention is paid to young women athletes' diets. At one girls' basketball tournament I attended in the Midwest, the teams ate at a cafeteria twenty miles from the gym because it was the cheapest spot. The players generally swallowed greasy fried chicken, heavy rolls, and chocolate cake before the games. At the Junior Olympics one summer in Lincoln, Nebraska, all of the athletes, from discus throwers to gymnasts, were housed in the empty dormitories at the University of Nebraska, and they ate their meals in one on-campus dining room. For those opposed to preservatives and junk food, it was easy to starve. One afternoon I was interviewing a diver who had a thirty-minute break before her next round and wanted something to eat. We set out to the athletes' snack bar —where hot dogs, potato chips, and popcorn were the only available fare. The vending machines featured candy and Lifesavers. "I can't believe they don't have granola bars," groaned the anxious diver. Finally, I flashed all the official badges and press passes I had and insinuated my way into the dorm kitchen, where I paid the cook fifty cents and retreated with an energy-boosting orange for the young girl. "If I ate what they gave us, I'd probably dive and never come up again," she said.

If you begin a regular sports program—like running, swimming, or bicycling—and don't seem to be progressing, there's a good chance that the oxygen-carrying cells aren't doing their job well because of insufficient iron. One woman who began a jogging program with several friends found that after two months they could run two miles without much effort, while she was walking more than half the distance. "I couldn't even break a ten-minute mile," she says, "and I figured that it was just as I'd always thought—I'm a rotten athlete." She was about to quit her daily groaning when a female neighbor happened to mention that she had just been through the same thing, and an iron supplement had given her noticeably more stamina. "The nice thing about women getting involved in sports," the jogger says, smiling, "is that all of a sudden we understand each other. The feebleness that male doctors would assume was normal for us really isn't at all."

The recommended daily allowance of iron for women is 18 milligrams; and during menstruation or for very active women, almost twice that much may be suggested. It's hard to get all that iron without eating ridiculous amounts of calories. Three ounces of chicken liver has 8 mg of iron, one-half cup of raisins or lima beans has 2.5 mg, three ounces of turkey has 5 mg, and one-half cup of dried apricots has 5.5 mg. Not all of the iron consumed gets absorbed into the body. Citrus fruits (or vitamin C) increase the absorption considerably. And while Popeye might have gotten strong from his spinach, most other people won't, since an acid in spinach keeps much of the iron from entering the system in an effective way. Using iron cookware actually bolsters the iron content of food, and many cereals and bread have iron added—usually to replace what has been lost in milling. A few years ago, kids could get a science lesson by holding a magnet over a bowl of one of the Kellogg's cereals and watching black flakes fly, but the blending process has since been changed. Members of one volleyball team keep a jar of desiccated liver in their training room and snack on the powder —which looks and tastes awful—after practices. A more palat-able solution is an iron pill or multivitamin with iron. Some men experience ill effects from too much iron, but that occurs very rarely in women. An estimated 5 percent of American women have mild iron deficiency, and while it sometimes seems that an unusually large percentage of women athletes suffer from this, that's probably only because the athletes notice any lack of energy more quickly than most.

Fat Problems

Psychologists generally agree that extreme overweight is often a sign of emotional or physical deprivation. Feeling unfulfilled in some aspects of her life (or fearing that condition), the over-weight woman calms herself by keeping well stuffed with food. A sport can serve the same purpose as eating: It's a physical gratification, a way of experiencing the body and fulfilling the craving for physical expression. This connection between the psychology of sports and the psychology of eating may be one reason why active women are rarely fat. "The only way I could diet during college was to swim while everyone else was at dinner," says a woman in her mid-twenties. "If I stayed in my

room or the library and tried to work, I got hungry and depressed. But when I was swimming, I never felt deprived."
There's a physical explanation for this, too. When the blood is
diverted to other parts of the body, the stomach isn't prepared
to digest food and so doesn't send signals that it's time to eat.
Sometimes the mind flashes time-to-eat signals because it is
searching for distraction. The ubiquitous coffee break is really
just a time for stepping away from the immediate pattern and
seeking diversion. Elementary school kids need similar refresh-
ment, only they call it recess.

Excess pounds, instead of being a disease in themselves, are
a sign that the system is out of balance. "There's no such thing
as excess eating," says Dr. Dorothy Harris, "only inadequate
activity." Dr. Jean Mayer has noted that the appestat, which
helps the body determine what and when to eat, operates most
efficiently in active people. So a weight-reduction diet will be
most effective if accompanied by exercise. Antagonists to this
theory point out that using up 3500 calories (or one pound)
through exercise isn't easy. It takes a four-mile run to burn up
just one doughnut and several games of tennis for a large apple.
But this reasoning is somewhat specious. One hour of walking/
running at a moderate pace burns up roughly 500 calories—
more than half a day's intake at a spa like the fashionable
Golden Door. Instead of spending $1500 a week not to eat, you
can spend an hour a day having fun. In addition, increased
movement causes deeper breathing, which results in more oxygen entering the body to fuel the metabolic fires. The improved
metabolism inspires more energy, which, of course, encourages
even more activity. This nonvicious circle means that the correlations between activity and calories used are more intricate
than most people suspect. The diet that adds pounds at the
typewriter won't necessarily do the same on the track, because
when the body is exercised, the metabolic rate becomes more
effective.

It's axiomatic among psychiatrists that overeating reveals
sexual frustration. Sometimes women overeat as an uncon-

scious means of negating sexuality and denying any interest in the body; they often lose weight when they take a new lover. Food provides security, being a tie to childhood and the mother who fed you, so it serves as a sedative to relieve anxiety and hyperactivity. But overeating eventually causes guilt rather than pleasure and becomes a means of self-punishment. The fact that professional athletes gain weight when they retire is often a sign of their despair and feeling of emptiness or loss. They begin looking for a replacement for the sensual fulfillment of sports, a way of appeasing their overly tensed bodies. Similarly, women often eat too much when they're at odds with their physical selves. Olympic diving champion Micki King recalls going on a "wild eating binge" the year she failed to defend her national title on the 3-meter board. "I spent three weeks going out and drinking beer until two in the morning," she says. "I went to dances and parties, and I drank and ate things that I never used to. I gained twelve pounds, and one morning I looked at myself in the mirror and said, 'Hey—what are you doing? Is this supposed to be *fun*?' It was one of those times when you take a deep breath and realize it's time to regain control of your life." By the time Micki went to the Munich Olympics, she had learned her lesson. "The other divers thought I was a goody-goody because I wouldn't go out to the Hofbräuhaus to have a few beers. I figured there was diving during the first eight days of the Games, and there'd be eight days left to raise hell. But shoot, I didn't even go to the Hofbräuhaus after I won. I hate eating too much, I hate drinking too much, and I hate feeling crummy in the morning. So why should I indulge by doing all the stuff I don't like? If I'm a goody-goody, at least I don't feel rotten about myself any more."

The biggest problem many women have in losing weight is trying to establish a new habit by sitting and telling themselves *not* to eat. The mind is more receptive to yeses than noes. Willpower is fine, but it's much easier to decide to *do* something than to concentrate on abstemiousness. One young writer recalls that her system of self-rewards involved getting up at the end of every completed page to munch on figs or cookies. She was gaining weight but couldn't seem to change the pattern. "Once I was working at a friend's house for about a week, and there wasn't any food around," she says. "So, when I'd deserve a break, I'd get up and do sit-ups or jumping jacks—in absolute desperation. I don't know why it seemed like such a natural substitute, but I've kept at it. I even get more energy that way than from nibbling."

When women become involved in sports, they tend to eat with more restraint simply because it's uncomfortable to move quickly when you weigh too much. "Even though I only swim for an hour, it changes what I do for the whole day," says a New Jersey woman named Michelle who joined a swim club the day she went on a diet and eventually lost eighteen pounds. "My hungry time is always about four in the afternoon, but when I know I have to be at the pool at six, I don't dare eat then or I'll feel too heavy in the water." Even though the last thing an overweight woman wants to do is put on a bathing suit, swimming is good exercise for someone with excess weight since the buoyancy of the water makes movement easy and prevents stress on muscles and joints. "I was always telling myself that I'd start swimming as soon as I lost some weight," says Michelle, "but I never quite got there. This time I decided to just go and figure that nobody there particularly cared what I looked like." One comforting thought for the reluctant is that the more you weigh, the more calories you use up during an activity. So in combining sport with diet, the first pounds get shed quickly.

Dietary slips or indulgences don't seem quite so devastating if atonement can be sought the next day by playing a little harder. For example, one day Jane Frederick decided to take a break from her rigorous schedule of daily workouts and graduate school courses and indulge her culinary fancies by baking an apple pie. Jane prides herself on always eating fresh foods and never touching anything from a can, so the ingredients in a Jane Frederick apple pie are obvious: fresh apples, honey, whole cinnamon. "But I was really tired, and when I opened the refrigerator, I discovered that my roommate had bought a Mrs. Smith's frozen crust. I hate to make pie crusts, so I just filled it and stuck the whole thing in the oven." Afterward, when Jane looked at the label, she realized that the crust was loaded with all the diglycerides and monoglutamates and hyphenated preservatives that exist. "I was horrified and worked out twice as hard the next day for penance," she says. "But I have to admit, that pie sure tasted good."

Food for Jocks

What's the perfect sports diet? Your body will be better off with a meal of wheat germ, fruit, and yogurt than with a Big Mac and fries, but whether that will make you set new records is hard to say. When Babe Didrickson Zaharias became the heroine of the 1932 Olympics, she was a great disappointment to the women's editors at newspapers because she didn't have any favorite recipes or special diets. The only "beauty" advice she'd offer young women was not to eat oily foods or gravy. "That's just hot grease with some flour or water in it," she explained.

Every day marathon swimmer Diana Nyad gulps milkshakes that contain several hundred calories (she burns them up quickly in the water) and she eats raw eggs and meat. She leaves her food uncooked, insisting that (1) it has more protein that way and (2) it's easier than cooking. Often the foods which are touted as being ideal for "quick energy" actually have an enervating effect. Chocolate bars and sugary drinks may provide an immediate surge by raising the blood-sugar level, but metabolic highs are invariably followed by lows that leave the body considerably weaker. A similar problem may occur if you have orange juice and nothing else for breakfast. You will have plenty of energy on the way to work because of the sugar boost, but by mid-morning, the blood-sugar level plummets, and you'll want a fix of coffee cake or Lifesavers to feel better again. To avoid the seesaw effect, try snacks with minimal amounts of sugar. Golfers on the pro circuit often have bags of dried fruit or mixed nuts in their lockers. For a special lunch or dessert, a banana split is fine—but instead of the normal gooey concoctions, pile yogurt, fruit chunks, and bran flakes over the split-banana base.

Many active women ignore the three-meals-a-day formula in favor of more frequent and less filling meals or snacks. Fruit and cheese are good for you, and the time saved in not cooking can go for training. Celery filled with peanut butter or a banana cut in half and spread with the same are fine for munching. Generally, keeping raw vegetables like celery, carrots, broccoli, and cauliflower cut and handy in the refrigerator is a good idea, possibly with a yogurt dip (plain yogurt, mustard, and a dash of Worcestershire sauce is one California favorite) for dunking. A woman from Cape Cod who decided to diet by swimming every day and eating large amounts of lettuce and carrots to assuage any hunger pains found that it's unwise to overdo any food. After a few weeks, she noticed the palms of her hands turning an orangish tint, and the color began to spread to the bottoms of her feet. The problem was an overdose of vitamin A, which can become toxic.[2] Her doctor advised that she give up carrots until the excess vitamin A stored in her body was gone.

Vegetables (eaten in normal quantities) are best when they're raw or cooked lightly so that the vitamins and minerals don't get boiled away. "I've really gotten into Oriental cooking," says one woman who plays tennis at a club in suburban Washington, D.C. "It's easy—you throw all sorts

2. Vitamins A, D, and E are fat-soluble and don't get readily excreted in the urine if they're taken in large doses. Vitamins B and C are water-soluble and don't get stored in the body, so there can be little danger from taking too much. However, taking one part of the B complex (i.e., B_1 or B_6 or B_{12}) in excess can drain the body of the other parts of the group.

of fresh vegetables into a wok, cook them briefly, and there you are." Along with a wok, the essential equipment for preparing naturally healthful foods seems to be a blender. Shakes are quick to make and easy to digest for a light sports meal. Favorite ingredients to toss into the mix include skim milk, yogurt, whatever fruit is available (apples, blueberries, strawberries, cantaloupe, bananas), wheat germ, orange juice, and ice cubes for texture. Athletes in high-energy sports may add malt or preparations like Sustagen, which is full of nutrients and calories. Fred Dryer, a football player for the Los Angeles Rams, consumes about seventy raw eggs a week in natural shakes that he blends fresh daily. He contends that eggs are the only wholesome food, and as long as they're not cooked, the cholesterol doesn't count. There's not a nutritionist around who agrees, but Dryer is thriving.

Plain food isn't enough for some athletes, who are always looking for new supplements, pills, and magic potions. The biggest supplement freaks are undoubtedly male bodybuilders; they would probably swallow hornets if they thought that would make them bulge more. One Mr. America told me that his nutritional program involved swallowing great quantities of protein powder, amino acids, liver tablets, multivitamins, B complex, glycerin, kelp, folic acid, and dolomite. And while he's not swallowing hornets yet, he's getting close and joining many other athletes in relying on Bee Power. Several health food companies are turning out bee-pollen pills, which are supposed to give busy athletes extra energy. Proponents drone on about the advantages of the pills, and the price of the tablets is very high—about forty-five dollars a pound. One teaspoonful, which gets compressed to one tablet, represents the work of six hundred female bees bumbling around in the flowers for an hour. Pollen is actually the sperm cells of flowering plants that bees collect for food. Far more men than women have been stung by the fad, so it's possible that the men are picking up the subliminal marketing hints that pollen is potency-inducing. A study conducted at Louisiana State University by Dr. John Wells concluded that swallowing bee pollen might give an athlete a mental buzz, but it doesn't do much else.[3]

At various times, vitamins C, E, and the extract lecithin have been touted as the magic that can improve energy, endurance, sex life, and body tone. The latest on the list is vitamin B_{15}. When *New York* magazine ran a cover story on vitamin B_{15}, calling it a wonder drug taken by many athletes, including Muhammad Ali, stores in the city sold out of it within days. The Federal Drug Administration and various state agencies across the country began to intervene, seizing shipments in some states and banning sales elsewhere. The alleged problem is that B_{15} isn't a vitamin at all—a vitamin is an essential dietary requirement—but rather a food additive that the FDA hasn't yet cleared. There's virtually no doubt that B_{15} is nontoxic, but orthodox drug companies want to keep it off the market, being suspicious of any chemical that is extracted from apricot pits.[4] Advocates claim that whatever label it's given, B_{15} increases the supply of oxygen in the blood and therefore improves endurance, cures anemia, and prevents angina attacks.

One competitive runner says she takes food supplements regularly, even though she's not sure that they do much. "It's a little like God," she says. "You can doubt that there's anything to it, but just in case it's true, you don't want to be caught not believing." For most, well-chosen foods provide all the

3. Dr. Wells divided the athletes on several university teams into groups, giving some ten pollen tablets daily, and others ten placebos. He concluded that there was absolutely no difference in metabolism or performance between the two groups.
4. Another substance extracted from the same source is Laetrile, which has been sold as a cure for cancer. It has been under fire from the FDA and banned in nearly all states. Substantive data on the effectiveness of Laetrile are virtually nonexistent. But there are data on B_{15}, and tests on Soviet rowers suggest that it may improve energy and prevent hardening of the arteries. B_{15} is taken seriously in several foreign countries, and athletes, notably in Russia, pop the pills in quantity. If it seems surprising that two such controversial substances should have been found in the same innocent apricot pit, there is a reason for the coincidence. Both were isolated by the same person.

energy they need. A good figure is usually one of the happy results of sports eating, since for most women, the weight at which they look best is roughly the same as the weight at which they'll do best in sports. Eating well becomes much easier when you're responding to how your body feels and moves rather than to how many pounds you have to lose to get into a smaller-sized dress.

Chapter Eight

Competition and Attitude

"Admirable woman! . . . Would you now prefer to be independent
and take the pole? I admit it is better fun to punt than to be punted,
and that a desire to have fun is nine-tenths of the law of chivalry."
(Lord Peter Wimsey)
—Dorothy Sayers

Everyone seems to know by now that exercise is good for you
and that it feels better to be fit than unfit, but women who want
to compete rather than just play are still caught in a quagmire
of uncertain attitudes. Having moved beyond the early stages
of women's sports, nobody is exactly sure how to continue.
Leaders of the women's sports movement (notably the executives of the AIAW) are torn between wanting respectability—
which, in men's terms, means playing for big stakes—and wish-
ing to avoid the pattern of corrupt competitiveness that has
characterized the men's activities. Athletic women who went to
college in the late 1950s remember with horror the "play days"
that took the place of competition for women. The field hockey
teams of, say, Vassar and Smith would meet, but rather than
squaring off against each other, the players would intermingle
for an afternoon's "recreation." Most women found it unbearably frustrating. "We'd be out there playing what should be a
competitive game, but we weren't allowed to take it seriously
or take any pride in winning," says one woman who is now a
college administrator. "You could never develop a sense of
teamwork because your teammates were always changing."

Even in the early seventies, the effort to keep women's sports pure teetered between the annoying and the absurd. Athletic scholarships were forbidden for women until the 1974-75 school year, and other restrictions effectively discouraged women from competition. Margie Shuer, a swimmer who eventually organized the women athletes at Stanford to demand some equity in the university's program, recalls that her swimming-team mates never attended the national championships. "The school officials said they had the responsibility to get the money to send us," she says. "But they wouldn't give us anything, so we said we'd pay for ourselves. They wouldn't let us do that either, because it wouldn't be fair to people on the team who couldn't afford it. It was just bullshit on top of bullshit until finally nobody could go." Later, when money was forthcoming, there were other obstacles. "The women were allowed to work out only in the spring and fall—not in winter because it was 'too cold,'" she says. "Of course, the men worked out all year round, so they were in top form for the nationals at the end of the winter season. I think the synchronized swim team had more pool time than we did."

When I was a freshman at Yale, the best way to qualify for a varsity sport was simply to be willing to play. The women's athletic teams were new, and nobody had yet thought to recruit female athletes. The captain of the women's gymnastics team had never been near a balance beam until she enrolled in a noncredit gym class, and most of her teammates came up the same way. That squad of neophytes had a more successful win-loss record than any of the highly recruited men's teams.

But it didn't take long for that everyone-can-play ethic of women's sports to erode. Seeing the money-making potential of women's events, administrators around the country began wooing talented high school girls with scholarships and promises of fame. Olympic basketball player Nancy Lieberman was probably the first to be hit by the new code: She had more than seventy college representatives pounding on her door when she was a senior in high school, with coaches appearing at all hours to make their pitches. Among the illegal inducements offered her were a car and an apartment. "This is called equality," one coach said with a shrug. "The men have been cheating for years."

The problem now is that the women are cheating themselves. With no other standard available, women have been trying to advance by emulation. "Equal" has been interpreted as meaning: Everyone will be like the men. But accepting that involves settling for women's rights when we could be demanding women's liberation. The former means slipping into roles that have already been defined by men in sports—roles that aren't necessarily desirable but that give new status. Yet why follow these silly rules when there's a chance to liberate everyone by making up new games? Because women have been so neglected in sports dealings, the chance to be like the men in control is a decidedly heady experience. But doing so means women will become enmeshed in the same abuses—the same over-commercialization and under-the-table dealings—that have characterized men's sports. At UCLA, athletic director Judith Holland is currently playing with a budget of more than half a million dollars, enough to make administrators of other women's programs complain that UCLA can buy athletes. "I cringe every time I hear about how much money we have," she says. "The men's budget is three and a half million, and compared to that, we have nothing." Too much sympathy for her plight is unnecessary. The desire to have sports available to women doesn't have to translate into programs with the same questionable priorities as the men's, where millions are poured into money-raising games that few can play but many watch.

It's time to raise a generation of participants, not another generation of fans. Holland claims that before long "women's basketball will become our football. It will have real status and be a revenue-producing sport." Great. Give it a few more years, and all the women who are now discovering the joys of movement and personal participation will be sitting in their living rooms sipping beer (or white wine) and watching a Sunday afternoon basketball game. But there are other possibilities, which presage a less chilling future. Phyllis Bailey at Ohio State wants a program in which a girl who gets a kick out of soccer has a chance to compete, and someone who has never held a field hockey stick can learn to play. When male administrators fought Title IX, claiming that it would destroy their programs, women tried to placate them by promising that no money would be siphoned away from the million-dollar men's events. It was a bad promise. Urging cuts in big-budget sports like football in favor of a more fairly distributed sports program for men and women could encourage everyone into activities which provide lifelong inspiration and pleasure, rather than a few years of glory. This isn't as much of a fairy tale as it may seem. As football becomes increasingly expensive, administrators at several schools have decided to salvage their athletic budgets by cutting the sport entirely. Despite initial trepidation, most of them are now glowing with success. Once the football monolith gets cut down, previously ignored sports— particularly those for women—flourish. One good example of this occurred at Pepperdine University in Malibu, California. With sunshine, beaches, and movie stars available, athletic director Wayne Wright realized that football was an unnecessary lure. "Football costs a fortune, and it's foolish for a small school to try to support it," he says. "There are enough professional teams around, and why should we be competing with them?" Some of the diverted funds at Pepperdine have gone into developing top-quality teams in women's volleyball, basketball, and tennis.

Inevitably, there is concern about the direction in which women's sports are headed, and one problem came into sharp focus in 1978, when the women's basketball team at UCLA won its first national championship. In the final round, UCLA played the University of Maryland before a packed stadium and NBC television cameras. The triumph was both a breakthrough and a warning that women's sports have arrived, but they have also changed. NBC had paid almost nothing for the broadcast

rights, but there were few complaints, since a year or two earlier, nobody was taking so much as a Polaroid to the women's
games. The fact that two large schools—traditional stalwarts in
men's sports—had made it to the championship round sent
chills of delight and consternation through the fans. From the
beginning, the women's championships had been dominated by
small schools, a situation which appealed to sentimentalists
with a romantic notion of parity. The emergence of the large
schools threatened the down-home atmosphere of the events
and suggested that women's sports were becoming just like
the men's. But one fact that was ignored in all this mourning for
lost innocence was that the large schools—with more students, facilities, and money—deserved to do well. Their earlier
floundering was simply a sign that they had failed in encouraging their women to be competitive. Critics lamented that the
small schools, which had long supported their women's teams,
were being turned into second-class citizens. But UCLA coach
Billie Moore insisted that there was another side to the issue.
"Women's sports have *always* been second class, or maybe
eighth class," she said. "This year, we were dedicated to changing that and running a first-class operation."

At most schools, nobody pays much attention to non-varsity
activities, and women are considered to be making strides only
when money is routed toward big-league sports. What needs to
be established is a balance, so that women will be neither exploited nor ignored in competitive sports. Top athletes are, of
course, an inspiration for everyone else, and providing opportunities for them is vital—as long as everyone else isn't forgotten in the process. Billie Jean King worries that women's sports
are still mired in hypocrisy—that the paucity of money and the
restrictions on college recruiting aren't signs of purity but of
continued stifling. "Women should be getting whatever they
can from sports in an open market," says B.J. "Believe me, it's
nice to be wanted, and that's what recruiting and big paychecks
are all about. It's like the way I feel when I'm being hassled by

reporters after a match. They can drive me crazy, but I love it —because nobody used to care about women athletes at all, and now they do."

But even as women begin to feel that they are doing just fine playing on new turf, the insidious discrimination grinds on. Girls still get channeled into cheerleading squads that stand on the sidelines yelling while the boys are on the fields playing. Since the advent of Title IX, several school principals have boosted cheerleading to a varsity sport. "That totally ignores the spirit of the law, which was supposed to open new activities to girls," says a female track coach. The leader of one cheerleading squad in Connecticut was amazed when the school administration gave her girls an additional $1000 for new uniforms and first-class travel with the football team. She was delighted at "all this support" until she realized that none of the other women's teams was receiving a cent. On paper, it looked as if the administration were doing wonderful things to advance girls' sports, but actually it was just dumping money into supporting the status quo. Usually when the status of women's sports goes up, the status of cheerleading goes way down. At a high school in Massachusetts, the women's athletic director refused to give the cheerleaders uniforms unless they agreed to cheer at the girls' athletic events. She wanted them to realize that being on the sidelines wasn't the best way to fulfill their potential. "Most of us felt a little silly cheering for the girls because it made us see that we could be out there playing ourselves," says the captain of the squad, who eventually joined a track team. "I guess we all grew up thinking it would be an honor to be a cheerleader, and never realized that there were other possibilities." When girls are cheering, the only ones really being honored are the male athletes. Cheerleading squads were initially formed so that girls could be involved—at least vicariously—with a team. Now athletic women deserve their own spotlight, not the reflected glory from the men.

The first crop of female athletes who have faced little discrimination and are motivated by much the same ends as the men is beginning to appear in the young tennis players on the girls' circuit. These girls have role models in Chrissie and Billie Jean and Martina, and many of them expect to reach superstar status before they reach five feet tall. Some already play less for fun than for the fame and commercial contracts that they expect will follow. Girls who lose too often may find their careers abruptly halted by disappointed mothers or financially troubled fathers. To understand the path that women's sports are rumbling down, I spent some time one summer at the junior national championships. At one of them, in Shreveport, Louisiana, some of the finest teenagers in tennis gathered. "If you do well here, you get a good ranking," explained a small, dark-haired girl named Karen, "and everyone's nice to you because they think you'll end up rich. If you get a bad ranking, you feel like junk."

Most of the mothers sitting at courtside admitted that they had expected to chauffeur their daughters to ballet class and piano lessons, not tennis tournaments. But they had gotten into the spirit quickly, feeling that talent with a tennis racket is a clear route to stardom for their girls. "Sure I'm living out my competitive instincts through my daughter," said one woman. "I never got to compete in my day, and I'm glad that she can. What's wrong with that?" A good deal was wrong. Though warned against interfering, mothers were constantly arguing line calls, challenging seedings, and complaining to the tournament director. For example, the mother of a top-ranked player from Florida seemed to feel that her daughter could never lose a match—only get cheated out of victory. In the quarter-final round, she watched while Susie, a quiet and sometimes sullen young girl, split the first two sets with her opponent, a spirited player with a mouthful of braces who had traveled to the tournament alone. "My mother cried when I left," she said, "but I like being on my own. It's fun being independent. Anyway, I'm the one who's playing, so I should learn what to do myself." The Florida mother thought differently and fretted as the two girls glared at each other across the net. During the ten-minute rest break before the third set, she pulled Susie into the locker room. "She looked so lethargic on the court," this mother confided to me. "I said to her, 'Honey, anyone watching this would think I'm the typical tennis mother, making you go out there and play. But I know you really want to win.'" She diagnosed the cause of the languor: The day was hot and slim Susie had eaten too much lunch. "It took me the full ten minutes to convince her that I should make her throw up. She kept saying, 'Mother, how gross.' Finally, I stuck my finger down her throat. She was crying and shaking, but she went back out there and won, and I know she was grateful."

The players' headquarters that year was the Chez Vous motor inn, and by 9:00 every night, the girls were all in their beds, and the motel was strangely quiet. The manager was surprised, having expected that a group of energetic fourteen-year-olds would spend most evenings tossing water balloons at each other or throwing their friends into the swimming pool. "Everyone is very serious," explained a long-haired girl from Michigan named Felicia. "Nobody fools around here. You spend every night in your room thinking about who you'll be playing and what you should do. You get so nervous that you can't even sleep. It's hard to relax, ever." The least maniacal youngster in the group was Tracy Austin, a guileless child who eventually won the tournament without losing a set. Tracy was on her way to becoming the youngest ever to play at Wimbledon, the U.S. Open, and on the professional circuit—a prodigy who had been weaned to be the next femme fatale of tennis. But she cheerfully tied her hair into pigtails and wore pinafore dresses with big bows designed by Little Miss Tennis. "At this age, the girls would rather die than have their nipples show," explained her mother, Jeanne. Tracy tried ignoring the jealousy-inspired rumors that circulated about her, and she only shrugged when people kept comparing her to the young Chris Evert. "We don't think about that," said Jeanne Austin, "and we're not rushing Tracy into anything. Maybe this will all fall apart in a year, but meantime, she just enjoys playing. Sometimes I want to protect her from hurt feelings, but I know it's something she has to face alone."

Few of the other mothers managed such calm, and most seemed to think that tennis was either a path to riches or a useless activity. "It sometimes seems like a cockfight here," said one mother from Connecticut. "We put yours and mine in the ring and watch them fight it out." But at all cockfights, someone has to get hurt, and with young competitors, the wounded are those who leave the court time after time in defeat and cultivate an image of themselves as losers. Many sour on sports, deciding that being number two or ten or ninety-nine out of the top one hundred is a humiliation they can't bear. Something has gone awry when that occurs, because the nerve and discipline and ease developed on the courts should give even the losers a self-satisfaction missing in their nonathletic, boy-chasing friends back home. Having a glimpse of a wide-open future, they're conscientious and goal-oriented. "I like the kids on the tennis circuit much better than the ones who go to my school," said one player. "The girls at home seem so silly. They're always wasting time and never try anything important."

Some of the parents understand that it shouldn't matter if their daughters turn pro or not, because through tennis they have at least learned about dedication and discipline, learned to put themselves on the line and work for a dream. "I didn't know anything about tennis, and all of a sudden someone at the club told me that Caryn was doing well," said Nita Schindler, a housewife from Baltimore. "I went crazy. I figured—my star! I have a star! Now I'm realistic. She's not the best one out there and she'll never win a fortune, but tennis is going to make her a real person. She's learning to take the hard knocks as well as the breaks. What more can I want from sports for my girl?"

Meshing competition and good spirit isn't an impossible task, and occasionally it can be done with flair. One example is the Colgate Women's Games, an annual event for inner-city girls in New York which represents a combined gesture of corporate image making and community good will. The possibly apocryphal story told by Colgate officials is that one morning in 1974, company chairman David Foster was flipping through the newspaper and read that Fred Thompson, coach of the renowned Atoms Track Club in Brooklyn, lacked the funds to take his girls to Europe for some international meets. Foster called Thompson into his office, casually wrote him a check for the trip, and asked what else Colgate could do for little girls who liked track and field. Together, they dreamed up the Colgate Games. That first year, the program attracted about five thousand participants. Then, like the Super Bowl, which also charts its progress with Roman numerals, the Games grew larger and more spectacular. By Games IV, about seventeen thousand young women were participating.

The main point of the Games is that everybody plays. Six-year-olds with baby fat waddle around the track, and girls twice their age get tips on race style and strategy from young women twice *their* age. Everybody wins something: a T-shirt, a certificate, maybe a $500 scholarship for the very best. For five weeks, even the losers aren't losers because they're urged to come back the next weekend and try again. "We think of this as a development program," says Thompson, "and the girls are hungry for it. They don't have anyplace else to run." The races are divided into age groups, from first graders to adults, and the participants get points (and medals) for finishing better than sixth place in any heat. After five weeks and some complicated computations, the top scorers are invited to the finals in Madison Square Garden, where cheering friends and television cameras greet them. Some of the greatest runners in the world have raced at the Garden, and the symbolism of being there isn't wasted on even the smallest girls. "They're learning that they can do something with their lives and be someone important," says Fred Thompson. "Track is just a way to reach girls and prove to them that if they work hard, they can be something special."

Around Brooklyn, Fred Thompson is known as The Saint. He

has changed the lives of so many young women that in Bed-ford-Stuyvesant, an area known for its street gangs, dropouts, and drug addicts, his phone number is scrawled on brick school walls under the spray-painted slogan: "Fred Saves." Most of his Atoms, like many of the girls at the Games, are black and live in the rougher neighborhoods of the city. Thompson's goal is to make them self-willed and strong at a time when they would normally be most vulnerable. He relentlessly teases the teenage Atoms about the men who ask them to go steady, reminding the girls to look at their boyfriends as equals, not saviors. "I want the girls to remember that they have some worth, too, and they don't have to grab a man and run away," he says. "Most black women in our society end up alone at some point, and they should be prepared for that. They have to be able to rely on themselves."

One of the first champs to emerge from the Atoms many years ago was Linda Reynolds, who, as a precocious fourteen-year-old, had developed enough to try out for the Olympics. Thompson was elated by this early success, but within two years, he discovered one of the agonies of coaching women: Sixteen-year-old Linda was pregnant. The story of what happens to a pregnant inner-city teenager gets repeated often: She drops out of school, marries a young man not ready to be a father, and begins an anguishing series of babies, divorces, fights, and abortions. For a while, it looked as if Linda wouldn't be any different. Her parents threw her out of the house, and she quit high school. Scared and forlorn, she turned to Fred for a place to stay. "I would have cracked up if not for him," she says now. "He stuck by me and insisted that this wasn't the end of my life. Fred Thompson has the purest motives of any man in this world. He's an honestly good human being." A month after her baby was born, Linda returned to daily practices with the Atoms. "Fred would hold the baby while I did workouts, and he'd be screaming, and the baby would be screaming, and I'd run around the track with a big smile. I got rid of all my tensions and frustrations by running, and each time around the track felt like I was rebuilding my life." Linda got a lot of mileage out of her running shoes, and she now has a college degree, a full-time job, and a good deal of confidence.

The Atoms team has won more national titles and set more records than any other club in the country, but Thompson has no idea how many medals his team members have won, and he won't bother counting. "Even if we'd never won anything, the Atoms would be a success. The Atoms is a social project. I don't devote myself to making champions—I'm concerned with saving young girls." The youngest, the L'il Atoms, train along with the most accomplished, and despite the constant competition, a spirit of good fellowship prevails. There are doctoral candidates and young businesswomen in the Atoms family, and their example has a special impact. For example, Cheryl Toussaint, who won a silver medal in the Olympics and works as an analyst at an investment firm, still works out with the Atoms. "She walks in the door after work, dressed immaculately and carrying a briefcase, and the other kids start imagining themselves just like her," says Thompson. "After all, they're changing in the same locker room and running on the same track, so why not? It's beautiful. I don't have to say a word, because they see what their lives can be like."

The Colgate officials see, too, and see that sports can change lives. After Games I and II, Colgate gave $1000 grants to local clubs that had supported girls and needed money for equipment and uniforms. In the following years, the results of the aid were apparent in the number of girls sporting warm-up suits inscribed with club names: Cougars, Jaguars, Jets, Dynamites. The grants are being continued. Many of the team coaches are fathers and mothers, and few have had much experience in track. But the hugging and spirit at the Games suggests that while only a handful of the girls will ever qualify for serious competition, the rest are learning that they can, at least, challenge the world on their own two feet. Competition doesn't have to be damaging. When the attitude of the participants is positive, so are the results.

Competition and Men

In the spring of 1978, three television crews and a score of reporters converged on a high school baseball field in Texas to watch Linda Williams play. The eighteen-year-old student went 0 for 2 at the plate and committed an error in the field that let four runs score. The otherwise ordinary game received national attention because Linda was making her debut on a previously all-male team and had been assured her spot in the lineup by a Federal court order. As she painfully found, representing all of womanhood on a baseball diamond is a singularly uncomfortable task.

The question of whether or not girls should stick with girls in sports has caused several imbroglios. In the mid-seventies it became clear that while there was separation in most sports, there was no equality, and several women defected from their teams to seek the right to play with the boys. The immediate worry was that this talent drain would keep the women's teams from improving. A welter of disparate regulations appeared: In some places women could compete on men's teams only if there was no equivalent activity exclusively for them; elsewhere schools experimented with having male, female, and coed teams in the same sport. Clearly much of the segregation in sports has always been unnecessary and destructive. Typical was the sports program in one elementary school outside Boston where the girls spent gym class during the spring playing dodge ball under the watchful eye of an English teacher who tottered on high heels and warned, "Be careful, girls. Not so hard!" The boys marched triumphantly past them to where the school's one male teacher taught them to play baseball or softball. In many grade schools, the boys and girls now play together, and the gym teacher—male or female—is hired specifically for that job, and wears sneakers. The arguments over whether this happy mixing should continue beyond childhood often get mired in almost unfathomable fatuity. When a judge in London ruled that a young girl from Nottingham had a right to play on a boys' "under 12s" soccer team, there was general panic among adult male officials, who wondered how they would know when a girl had gotten old enough so that playing with the boys was indecent.

Allegedly looking out for women's best interests, many coaches claim that if teams are mixed, all of the women will end up sitting on the bench. It's true that very few women—even the superathletes—could qualify for a men's football team; in many sports, women should compete against women so that skill rather than size determines the winners. But sometimes the aim of segregation is to preserve machismo rather than to benefit women. For example, one of the more breathtaking events in sports is the cliff-diving championship held annually in Acapulco. Competitors perch on a jagged cliff almost ninety feet above the sea, then plunge forward into what they hope will be twelve feet of water. Misjudging a wave or failing to propel themselves far enough away from the rocks portends disaster. For two years in a row, Barbara Mayer Winters of Arlington, Texas, went to Acapulco to dive. After being sent away the first year, she returned in 1978 on a honeymoon with her husband, Rick, and was allowed to mount the cliffs enough times to become one of only three Americans to qualify for the finals. But that was it. The Mexicans threatened to quit if Barbara was in the finals, so she was disqualified. There were a few chivalrous protestations about Barbara's safety but they were merely rhetorical. One Mexican understood the real complaint. "This is a death-defying activity," he said. "The men are taking a great gamble to prove their courage. What would be the point if everyone saw that a woman could do the same?"

One of the few sports in which men and women have competed together in international meets is rifle shooting. Margaret Murdock, a chunky anesthesiologist from Topeka, Kansas, became the first woman to win an Olympic medal in the sport, in 1976. Each "course of fire" in the competition lasted for over five hours, and Margaret unnerved many of her opponents with her steely skill. "A woman can't tolerate the pressure of shoot-ing," Margaret says laughingly. "At least, that's what they tell me." She came so close to winning a gold medal (taking the silver instead, on a scoring fluke) that when the national an-them was played at the awards ceremony, the male winner asked her to step up and stand next to him, sharing the honor. Among those watching the proceedings was Margaret's five-year-old son.

Such incidents don't always soften male opposition to women in sports, and in fact, they sometimes exacerbate it. Men are happiest if they can surround women athletes with a "Gee whiz, look what she can do and she's only a girl" aura. So, in fluff promotions like CBS-TV's "Challenge of the Sexes," top women athletes are given generous handicaps to compete against top men. That way, even if they win, the women are losers. But mixed competition is valuable only when it provides a way of asserting the female self without apology. In sports where it's reasonable, the point is for women to be competing not *against* men but with them, as equals.

Before women could play Little League in New Jersey and soccer in London and baseball in Texas, someone had to make a statement about female power. There's no other way to de-scribe the Billie Jean King vs. Bobby Riggs tennis match played on national TV in 1973. This was Man against Woman, and the outcome was somehow going to determine whether Woman even had a right to be on the big-time court. With all the pomp and ceremony that surrounded the match, the scores of cham-pagne-sipping celebrities who ringed the court, and the thou-sands of fans who filled the Houston Astrodome, the last thing that really concerned anybody was tennis. But when it hap-pened that Woman won, nobody could ignore the symbolism that spoke through all the silliness.

The real issue in mixed competition is whether men and women can respect each other as professionals and as individu-als. Women aren't just lovers, sex symbols, and wives, and the best way for men to realize that is to deal with them in situations where romance is not the prime consideration. Men's difficulty in dealing with this became apparent during the Great Locker-Room Controversy, which reached a fervid pitch at the 1977 World Series when baseball commissioner Bowie Kuhn banned female reporters from the locker rooms. When one magazine reporter screamed "discrimination," Time, Inc., brought a lawsuit against Kuhn, who cheerfully admitted that the reporter was banned "by virtue of her sex" but added that allowing women into men's locker rooms would be an invasion of privacy. The irony is that the postgame locker-room antics were broadcast on television. It's hard to understand how one woman constitutes "invasion of privacy" while television cameras don't. "Most of the guys on the team aren't exhibitionists," said Tommy John, the player representative for the Los Angeles Dodgers, a team that had voted to allow women into their World Series chambers until Kuhn vetoed the idea. "It's not a hardship to pull on a towel when you come out of the shower. I don't parade around naked even in front of male reporters." Baseball officials weren't the only ones trying to keep women as far away from sports as possible. Just a few years earlier, women were barred from press boxes at ball parks and football stadiums and weren't even allowed into sports banquets or some writers' associations.

Reducing everything to sex roles is demeaning. A sweaty, smelly, noisy locker room is not the place for amorous encounters, and tossing a ball to a woman teammate is one pass that isn't meant to lead to bed. Women and men should be able to deal with each other at many different levels. "When the antifeminists say they want men to look at them as women, I don't know what they mean," says one woman who led a local fight for the Equal Rights Amendment. "I assume they don't want to sleep with every man they meet. But if that's the only way a man can see a woman, it makes any other interaction impossible." That kind of one-edged perspective is often the only reason for keeping women and men apart in casual sporting circumstances. In neighborhood leagues, office or company competitions, and intra-college skirmishes, the concept of *people* playing together should prevail. "Playing with someone else's husband at our tennis club is seen as a cause for gossip," says one woman from suburban Philadelphia. "The whole setup makes me sick. The women's movement hasn't meant a thing until a man and woman can at least play tennis together without everyone assuming sexual overtones." Keeping women and men separated in sports is rather like the nineteenth-century habit of sending the ladies upstairs to chat after dinner while the men retired with brandy and cigars. Expecting a tennis game to change venerable patterns may be excessive, but sports do offer a likely place to begin. A man who is unaccustomed to relating to women in any but the most conventional ways gets a severe jolt when a female acquaintance becomes a sports opponent or teammate. Suddenly the flaring emotions of sports —the excitement, anger, or intensity—break through the facade he normally reserves for impressing women.

Single-sex competition does have the advantage of offering women the female equivalent to the male-bonding that men have always known. "The best part of rugby is that afterwards we all go out and drink and sing bawdy songs," says a member of a Boston women's rugby team. "We're together in a way women have never been before." A woman who plays on a softball team in California delights in a similar female team spirit. "About twice a week after games we go to a little pub and talk and eat and laugh. It's one time when you don't need a date. Or you can have one along, if you want, it really doesn't matter. What's incredibly special is that whoever's there—male or female—there's never any pretense or flirting." That this can occur bodes well, though some women will still have to infiltrate male ranks before full equality is achieved; when the boys have all the marbles, girls who want to play have to cut in on the game before they can expect a share of their own. It's inevitable that fairly soon, some woman will make her move to play professional baseball. After mad ravings and speeches on morality from the traditionalists, she'll qualify for the Dodgers or Yankees. Only then will other women think about forming their own league, confident of what they can do.

Women's sports have been developing from the top ranks down. The champions fight lonely battles until other women see the possibilities and follow their example. Unfortunately, the pioneers often view themselves as anomalies and identify their achievements as malelike. "I've exploited my own talents, but I don't think many other women could do this well," says gymnastics coach Muriel Grossfeld. "I've succeeded by dedication, hard work, concentration, and late hours. How many other women could work this hard without getting sidetracked?" Similarly, diver Micki King trained with men until she won her gold medal in the Munich Olympics, and immediately after that, she retired from competition to become the first woman coach at the Air Force Academy. Coincidentally, the year the academy finally began accepting women students, Micki asked for a transfer so she could follow her new husband while he attended flight school. "I don't think of myself as part of the women's sports movement because I've always been surrounded by males," she says. As an undergraduate at the University of Michigan, Micki was manager of the men's swimming team, where her official duties included picking up towels and doing laundry. She complied, since it gave her the chance to hang around the men's pool. The coach, Dick Kimball, risked his job for Micki and let her train with his team. "The men's athletic director was so opposed to women that whenever he walked by the pool, I had to hide," says Micki. "I don't know what I would have done without Dick—I think the diving board at the women's pool was condemned." Now, however, the University loves to claim Micki as one of its "daughters" and school brochures speak proudly of her. Similarly, after her Olympic triumph, her childhood hometown of Pontiac, Michigan, had a Welcome Back Micki King Day. "I didn't think anybody knew I'd left," she says.

Micki considers herself a traditional woman who was forced

to be unconventional because she happened to love sports. Since there were rarely women around her, she was convinced that personal female commitments and competition couldn't mix. "I compartmentalized my life, but I don't see how else I could have done it," she says. She met her husband, Jim Hogue, when she was a captain in the Air Force and he was a cadet, ten years and many stripes her junior. They dated surreptitiously for a year, until he received his commission. When I ran into Micki shortly after her honeymoon, her transformation to obsequious wife was disquieting to observe. "I was ready to stop being different," she said when I commented on the change. "People see me on TV and think I'm some kind of special person, but I see myself as ordinary. I'm just a wife, and I'm new on the job." Competing with men in the military and hailed as "the only woman" wherever she went, Micki had apparently felt vague quiverings under her militaristic pose. As soon as it was possible, she wanted to affirm her female-wife role. During a speech to a group of women coaches shortly after her honeymoon, Micki, who had been an inspiring example for many women, began making jokes about women's liberation. "When I was asked to join all those bra-burning organizations, I had to turn them down because I thought my contribution would be too small," she said with a sly smile. After the speech, two red-faced coaches approached Micki and angrily accused her of a demeaning attitude toward women.

Because of Micki's Olympic reputation, she didn't have any trouble coaching the men on the Air Force team. "They thought of me as a god, not a woman," she says, "so they could accept me as a coach—someone to hold in awe. I'm not sure they could have accepted me as a teammate." But women's sports will have done their part to advance male-female interaction only when there's an easy acceptance at all levels. For many of Micki's successors, that's beginning to occur. "I wouldn't think of keeping the men and women apart during practice," says diving coach Ron O'Brien with a smile. "Nobody gets ill at ease, and there are a lot of advantages. Certain dives are considered very difficult for women, but mostly the girls are just scared of them. When they see the men doing them day in and out, they begin to seem very routine. The women are a good influence on the guys, too, because they always give one hundred percent mentally and keep the men on an even emotional keel." There are advantages outside the diving room, too. "We're not supposed to fool around with the girls at night because there might be a lot of talk," says one of the male divers, "but we manage to be discreet and Ron looks away." On other swimming and diving teams, the situation is similar. Being part of a team doesn't preclude affection, though it is a signal for honesty and candor. "Sure I date the girls who swim with us," says one Florida athlete. "I see them all the time, so we're comfortable together. I guess the only difference is that I'm not trying to impress them, and I don't give them lines."

Standard notions about men, women, and competition were given a new twist shortly after women were first admitted to the U.S. Military Academy. The directors of the West Point office of military leadership expected that the prettiest and least threatening women would garner the most dates and warmest welcome from the men. But it didn't work that way. "Women cadets are accepted by male cadets largely according to how well they do in physical training," says one West Point officer. "The women who are best able to compete and compare with the men receive the most support and consideration." The first year, women were integrated into a dozen of the Academy's companies while the remaining two-thirds were still all male. The men in the all-male regiments continued to complain about having women in the corps, while the cadets in the integrated companies had no gripes. They were able to transform the abstract "indignity" of training with women into the agreeable fact of working and playing side-by-side with Katherine and Laura and Kelly. "Sometimes the men from other companies would ask us for a date just to see what it would be like," says one female cadet, "but basically we got closest to the men who trained with us." When the Army's first women's basketball team took to the court, even some of the previously belligerent men mellowed and lined the gym with signs reading "GO, SUGAR SMACKS." (West Point men are called smacks. They added the sugar for the sweeties.) One of those in the stands was a male upperclassman who had been outspokenly antagonistic about the admission of women, but he saluted and cheered when the women began to play. "I don't like the idea of having women at West Point," he said with the touch of a smile, "but athletes fighting for the school honor are another matter entirely."

Ultimately, women ought to be competing with men whenever they want. In 1978, an Ohio Federal judge ruled that girls can't be banned from contact sports like football, hockey, or wrestling just because they're girls. Some men balked at the ruling, but Judge Carl Rubin was firm. "It may well be that there is a student today in an Ohio high school who lacks only the proper coaching and training to become the greatest quarterback in professional football history," he wrote. "Of course, the odds are astronomical against her, but isn't she entitled to a fair chance to try?"

Chapter Nine

Moving On

What is certain is that hitherto woman's possibilities have been suppressed and lost to humanity, and that it is high time she be permitted to take her chances in her own interest and in the interest of all.
—Simone de Beauvoir

Since I began following sports several years ago, I've been collecting file drawers full of stories about women's achievements and struggles. Now there are more of these stories than ever before. Everyone I meet seems to have a niece who competes in ice hockey or a sister who runs hurdles or a mother who is taking a course in yoga, for goodness sakes. The stories run from the obscure to the significant. There is, for example, the twenty-nine-year-old woman who recently traveled around the world alone in a sloop. Her proud husband met her at the harbor 272 days and 30,000 miles after she began. A new record. Then there's the twelve-year-old schoolgirl who climbed Mount Snowdon on stilts, and the mother from Connecticut who frequently runs in long races while her quadruplet toddlers watch. The headlines always refer to her as "marathon mother." I reread these stories now and again to marvel at what women who become intrigued with sports of all kinds can do.

Attitudes have changed quickly. In city sandlots, there are as many girls lurking beneath baseball caps as boys. Girls in a few sports now accept equality as the norm and barely understand that less than a decade ago, a few brave pioneers were fighting for recognition. For example, an heiress apparent to Billie Jean

King is Pam Shriver, who made it to the finals of the U.S. Open when she was all of sixteen. Earlier, she had captured the top spot on the boys' tennis team at her private school in Maryland, and throughout her high school career, she recorded only two losses, both in the state championships. We were chatting together one day when I asked how the guys had responded to losing to her. She looked bewildered for a moment. "Well, nobody likes to lose," she said. Which was obviously the only important point.

Not all matters have evolved so gracefully. A young girl from New York spent many months trying to convince state educators to change the rules that banned her from playing on the boys' soccer team in her high school. Valerie had spent most of her growing-up years in South America and was certainly qualified for the squad. It took endless legal threats and a good deal of publicity to get the rules changed, but Valerie finally made the team. Joy! The next year, Valerie found that insidious discrimination doesn't respond to lawsuits. She was harassed before and after practices, and teammates refused to pass the ball to her. Even though Valerie scored her team's only goal in a preseason game, the coach still wasn't eager to have her around. When the season roster was posted the next day, Valerie's name wasn't included. The joy diminishes.

Knowing whether or not to be sanguine about women's current position in sports is difficult. It's confusing, at times, trying to understand exactly what is going on and why. For example, one sport that is being developed at a startling rate is racquetball. Court clubs are being built around the country, and the standard process of TV coverage, marketing sprees, and big promotions is under way. As with a few other new sports, a major push is being made to attract women. Nearly all of the new court clubs have free nursery facilities so young mothers can play without worrying about babysitters, and executives of the United States Racquetball Association say they're trying hard to get more women swinging. "Finances demand that at least forty percent of the market in a participant sport be women," says a manager of one sports manufacturing company. "So you can bet we're trying to attract the ladies any way we can."

All this left me with a happy glow, since racquetball is a good sport—it's easy to learn, fast-paced, and fun—and I'm occasionally willing to overlook motives when the results are so positive. But with a little more investigation, I found that all is not shining in this racquetball heaven. The problem is money, and the scenario is an old one: Women being underpaid and fighting for financial equality. On the professional racquetball circuit, women receive about one-third as much prize money as the men. Since the sport is new, the money available is limited, but that doesn't explain the grossly unfair distribution. At a recent national championship Shannon Wright, an outstanding female player, took home $3500 for winning, while the top man was awarded $10,000. The tournament was held at one of the high-quality *Sports Illustrated* court clubs, which are licensed by Time, Inc. Henry Luce, III, the vice-chairman of Time, was mostly silent when I asked him to discuss the subject. "I can't explain the great disparity in prize money, though it's probably not desirable," he said. Most of the women affected get somewhat more heated about the issue. The situation is particularly puzzling because Colgate-Palmolive—generally a guardian angel for women's sports—is the main sponsor of the tour. I have no doubt that this inequity will change rapidly. Some of the equal-rights-oriented executives of Colgate will begin to wonder about the ridiculous condition. Or the women will decide to pull away from the men and organize their own, better-paying pro tour. But the sameness of the circumstances becomes tiresome. How often must we return to square one to achieve another "breakthrough"? When will it happen that events proceed smoothly and equitably without a new fight each time?

A feminist friend of mine claims that men recognize in women's sports a final challenge to sexual domination, and each time they're faced with that possibility, their instinct is to rebel.

Whether or not that's true, it's undeniable that many of the struggles in the women's movement concern control of the female body. While it seems axiomatic that the power in these matters should rest with women, the reality is somewhat different, as men appropriate the authority that women don't always have the courage to establish. Though this responsibility may be unsettling for some, in sports there can really be no issue: Women must control their own bodies.

Women who begin a sport rarely regret it. At a recent New York City marathon, some of the loudest cheers at the finish line were reserved for the several hundred women who completed the race. Afterward many of the finishers hobbled over to the medical area, where they were treated for exhaustion or cramps. Others, like June Beltran Chan, a young Hawaiian athlete with an impressive marathon history, were carried there. "After twenty miles, I lost all sense of distance and time," said June when she recovered. "I was just driving myself to go on. I knew that wherever I stopped finally, I'd collapse." Her straight black hair, which hangs well below her waist, was soaking wet from the effort. "I feel very free when I run, with my hair flying behind me," she said dreamily. "I'm aware of heat, sun, blue sky, and black road. All my senses are aroused, and no matter what the weather, the day is beautiful."

Lying on a nearby cot was a novice runner, a slim redhead named Lisa Edmondson, who was shouting in pain from the cramps in her legs. A model and Wellesley College graduate, Lisa was smiling when her anguish subsided. "I'm lying here hurting, but I'm really pleased," she said. "I began running only a few months ago, and before that, I was the cloddiest, least athletic person you can imagine. Someone told me I hadn't trained long enough to run a marathon, and maybe that's why I got these cramps. But it doesn't matter, because I'm so happy, you wouldn't believe it. I've always competed in academics and modeling because I knew I could do well. But sports I do just for me. It's wonderful how that makes you feel. I set my goal, and I've reached it. And nothing else matters right now."

Some of the folderol which has characterized women's sports is beginning to diminish, and there's new respect for the physically capable woman. When twenty-one-year-old Nancy Lopez won five major tournaments in a row during her rookie year, she attracted headlines and galleries for the women's golf circuit that all the earlier sex ploys and come-ons had failed to draw. Nancy's natural, friendly manner and impressive displays of skill brought admiration rather than ogling. Fans were coming out not just to see a woman, but a woman golfer. "I like to look pleasant on the fairway," Nancy told me, "but that's not as important as how I play. I've never thought of myself as someone who could be sexy. I'd rather wear pants than short skirts, because I figure that when people come to watch me, they don't particularly want to see my rear end."

Women are finding that there are really very few reasons to stay away from sports. The Tennis Lady clothing shop in a fashionable section of Madison Avenue in New York City recently displayed in the window a mannequin wearing a maternity tennis dress. "I don't know if anybody else carries maternity tennis dresses," said the store manager, "but we sell a lot of them. We have them in about a dozen styles. You can wear them through the ninth month." Meanwhile, designers for Speedo, the swimsuit company, were working on a special maternity racing suit. They were inspired when Wendy Boglioli, a New Jersey swimmer in her mid-twenties, decided to enter a 1978 national championship when she was five months pregnant. Neither her condition nor her age could hold her back. Previously, women swimmers were thought to be washed ashore competitively in their teens. But women don't peak biologically until their twenties in some sports and their thirties in others. Now, with incentives like college scholarships and increased recognition, women are realizing that there's no reason to quit. They can survive puberty quite nicely and keep improving in sports.

When I speak about women's sporting potential, I'm often asked if my conclusion is that there's no difference between what men and women can do. I think the question is largely irrelevant. We're hardly at the point where it's necessary to argue about specific points of sameness or lack of it between the sexes. I generally accept the studies, notably those of Dr. Jack Wilmore, that suggest that under optimal conditions, there would be a 5 percent difference between men and women in terms of strength, and therefore of athletic performance. Even now, the difference between the top athletes of both sexes is no more than 10 or 15 percent. But what upsets me is that among most of us in the nonjock population, this small gap gets enlarged to an abyss—a 50 percent differential. I think of that as a 40 percent potential "sameness" which is misused and ignored. If we concentrate on what we can't do, we invite failure; if we believe in equality, it comes within our grasp. I'd rather hear women overemphasize their potential than abandon themselves to a limiting stereotype.

It was an impossibly hot and sultry day in Freeport, Bahamas, where I had gone alone for a four-day running workshop. There were five women in our group and one man—half of us were under twenty-five and single, the others under thirty-five and divorced. Teasing each other and following our coach, Mike Spino, we novices had run more than we had thought possible and had felt better and better doing it. Now we were going to be timed in a mile run. Not a race, Mike explained, just something to assay our skill so he could give us a fitness program to take home. Still, my heart was pounding at the starting line when it struck me that this was the first race of my life.

Two members of our group sprint out far ahead, while the rest of us settle into a comfortable pace. Running directly behind me is Penny Hill, a twice-divorced businesswoman in her early thirties who has left her six-year-old son at home. "This is the first vacation I've ever taken alone," Penny has told me. "Usually I want someone along to protect me from the pick-up scene at resorts, but I figured if I was at a running workshop, I'd have the guts to be myself." Penny and I have assured each other that we never run competitively and that we were active only for the fun of it. As we run now, I hear her breathing hard behind me, and it's a comfortable bond between us. Halfway through the last lap, Penny spurts ahead, but I'm unfazed, knowing that I don't have to compete with anybody. But if she can go faster, why can't I? With a deep breath, I surge past Penny, worrying for a moment that I'll use up all my energy and collapse in an embarrassed heap. But I don't, and we both pick up the pace, the lead changing several times. We cross the finish line exactly together, and throw our arms around each other, as if we'd just broken the four-minute mile. We haven't broken seven minutes, but it doesn't matter. Mike comes over smiling, and suddenly embarrassed, Penny and I joke with him about the slow time and our silly display. He shakes his head. "It was beautiful to watch," he says. "Most people don't understand that what they do in sports, at their own level, can be as perfect as a world record."

Stanley Keleman, a psychologist who has been studying body-mind interactions, once explained to me that in working with your body "you allow yourself to be moved. You experience yourself in a new way—different from all that goes on at a conscious level." It may sound mystical to claim that the body has its own knowledge and power to change a life, but anyone involved in sports understands that rational decisions don't always count for very much. "Our notion of 'knowing' has produced generalized misery," says Keleman. "When we learn to make the organism responsive, it is no longer as necessary to know." Well-considered decisions and rational plans are only the beginning. To understand yourself on a deeper level is more difficult, and the point of getting in touch with the body through sports is to discover who you are and what you can become.